DESERT

THE CALIFORNIA DESERTS

THE CALIFORNIA DESERTS
A VISITOR'S HANDBOOK

By EDMUND C. JAEGER

With Chapters by

S. STILLMAN BERRY and
MALCOLM J. ROGERS

STANFORD UNIVERSITY PRESS
STANFORD, CALIFORNIA

LONDON: GEOFFREY CUMBERLEGE
OXFORD UNIVERSITY PRESS

STANFORD UNIVERSITY PRESS
STANFORD, CALIFORNIA

LONDON: GEOFFREY CUMBERLEGE
OXFORD UNIVERSITY PRESS

———

THE BAKER AND TAYLOR COMPANY
55 FIFTH AVENUE, NEW YORK 3

HENRY M. SNYDER & COMPANY
440 FOURTH AVENUE, NEW YORK 16

W. S. HALL & COMPANY
457 MADISON AVENUE, NEW YORK 22

———

PRINTED AND BOUND IN THE UNITED STATES
OF AMERICA BY STANFORD UNIVERSITY PRESS

First Edition 1933
Revised Edition 1938
Third Printing 1941
Fourth Printing 1946
Fifth Printing 1948

PREFACE

So many travelers, vacationists, and students of nature are now interested in our California deserts that there seems to be a place for a practical handbook which they can use to help them understand what they see in this land of natural wonders. What I present is not a book of prospectors' tales or of aesthetic impressions and moods, but one rich in the information needed to make the traveler's mental picture of the desert a pleasant and at the same time a correct one, broad in scope and based on the findings of modern science.

I have been aided in bringing this work into its final form by the devoted zeal of two of my students, Mr. Willis Pequegnat and Mr. Howard Johnson, to whom I wish to express at the outset my deepest sense of gratitude. Dr. S. Stillman Berry, eminent authority on mollusks, has contributed a chapter on snails; and Malcolm J. Rogers of the San Diego Museum has written in his usual authoritative and pleasing style on the Indians. It would be hardly possible here to acknowledge by name all of the many friends who have aided in supplying information or in making suggestions and criticisms. Likewise it would be wearisome to the reader to list the reference works I have consulted and the authors to whom I am therefore under obligation.

The flower illustrations are all my own work and were made from living plants. Mr. W. A. Sharp made the delightful drawings in ink which head the chapters and which add atmosphere to the pages. Miss Pauline Hearst did the animals and the jacket design.

EDMUND C. JAEGER

RIVERSIDE, CALIFORNIA

v

We can enjoy things more, the more we know about them. Simply to be able to call the elements of beauty by their right names helps us to relive them. Intellectually to grasp an object of enjoyment is to possess it more securely. We take more pleasure in the stars if we know their names. We listen better to birds if we can distinguish them. We hear a symphony with deeper absorption if we know something of its harmonies.

—WALTER RUSSELL BOWIE
in "On Being Alive"
(quoted by permission of
Charles Scribner's Sons)

CONTENTS

ILLUSTRATIONS

CHAPTER I

INTRODUCTION

LORD BRYCE has said that "Renunciation is the hardest part of travel," and I would add that discovery is its greatest joy. And so, while I have made this a guidebook for the desert traveler, I have tried not to make everything so obvious and plain as to remove the enchantment of novelty or the joy of seeking for hidden treasure. I have told about many of the things there are to discover, but have left it for the reader to detect where the nuggets lie ensconced.

The geographical, geological, and other natural history features of our desert domains are so varied and with them are bound up so many entrancing problems that twenty years of intimate acquaintance and wide travel over the arid Southwest have not desiccated my ardor for continued study and wide wanderings nor lessened my eagerness to lead others to the heart of my kingdom of joy.

The question "What is a desert?" cannot be answered without facing many difficulties. The term desert does not necessarily imply paucity of life, continuous heat, marked lack of moisture, or the presence of sandy wastes, although all of these phenomena may occur. Even meagerness of rainfall is not always the deciding factor in the making of deserts but is only one of a combination of factors. Rocky or alkaline soils and continuous winds are features which play no minor rôle.

For our present purposes, deserts may be defined as places of high, diurnal, summer temperatures, with more or less steady, drying winds and slight rainfall (generally under five inches a year) and that unevenly and, from the standpoint of all but specialized plants and animals, often very unsatisfactorily distributed.

A little map study will reveal the fact that a surprisingly large portion of the globe is desert or semi-desert. Deserts have avoided the equatorial area and have chosen to lie "a little to the north of the northern tropic and a little to the south of the southern tropic" (Buxton). They constitute two broad belts lying for the most part directly under the trade winds and extending well across the continents. It is these trade winds that furnish the most important cause of deserts. Of great regularity and always athirst, they sweep over the lands and rob them of their moisture. The deserts of Southwestern United States lie north of the belt of trades but are visited by off-shore winds of the upper atmosphere, which are equally powerful causes of aridity. In December the south and southwesterly winds begin to bring rains to the Pacific Coast, but their moisture is largely dissipated by the lofty mountains before they reach the desert.

The largest of all deserts, the great Palearctic, stretches with certain minor interruptions from the Atlantic shores of northern Africa to northwestern India and far into the center of China. It includes the great Sahara, the deserts of Arabia, Iran, Turkan, and Takla Makan, and the Gobi. The second largest arid area comprises the enormous interior plains of Australia, sometimes spoken of as the dead heart of the continent. Next in extent are the North American deserts, occupying much of the Great Basin; reaching west and south they extend almost to the California coast and into Mexico.

Minor but much specialized deserts exist in southwestern Africa, in eastern Patagonia, in western Argentina, in the provinces of Atacama and Antofagasta in Chile, and in southern Peru. Each desert is to some extent the counterpart of every other; they have much in common. Each is an interior basin of irregular relief, surrounded, at least in part, by mountain masses or high plateaus which serve as barriers denuding the incoming winds of their moisture. In the midst of each of them are inland seas or lakes, and not a few have areas which dip below the level of the sea. The Caspian, the Dead Sea, and the Sea of Aral lie in the deserts of Asia; Great Salt Lake and the Salton Sea in arid North America; and Lake Eyre in the interior of Australia.

The area here treated embraces both the Mohave (Mohah'vay) and the Colorado Desert of southeastern California and also certain contiguous portions of southern Nevada and western Arizona, all within the realm of the creosote bush, that remarkable plant which marks better than any other the domain of the real American desert.

The Colorado Desert includes not only the area immediately contiguous to the Colorado River but also the Salton Basin and the rather low-lying bordering areas which drain into the Salton Sink. This agrees well with the conception of W. P. Blake, who first gave the Colorado Desert its name in 1853. From the biological standpoint the northern limit of the Colorado Desert may be arbitrarily placed as far north as a line drawn from the Morongo Pass easterly to the Colorado River. The Mohave is a high, somewhat quadrangular-shaped desert with an altitude varying from 2,000 to well over 5,000 feet. Except for a small area along the Colorado River, none of the waters which fall upon it reach the ocean but sink into the desert sands to be evaporated by the unremitting, dry, and often hot winds. Its western and southern boundaries are the San Gabriel and San Bernardino Mountains. To the north and east it stretches up into the Death Valley area and across the broad basins of eastern California into southeastern Nevada. The transition from one desert to the other is gradual but none the less definite, as is shown by the changing flora and fauna. To understand the differences these deserts show in physiography, climate, and plant and animal life, we must inquire as fully as possible into the peculiar history of their past.

CHAPTER II

THE DESERT'S PAST

THE desert's geologic history is one long series of changes. Deposits of limestones, sandstones, and other fossil-bearing rocks scattered widely but particularly evident in the far eastern and northern Mohave indicate that in ancient geological times (Cambrian and Carboniferous) much of the region was at least twice covered by the sea.

After these ancient periods of sea submergence the land was upraised, forming a high upland area of bold relief. But the erosive agencies of wind and water, both during the upheaval and afterward, were busy and during the long succeeding ages wore the country down until only broad lowlands diversified by hills and mere ridges were left. During periods designated by the geologists as early and middle Tertiary, volcanoes burst forth and repeatedly covered the land far and wide with deep accumulations of lava, mud, and ash, the remains of which are still widely seen. Volcanic outbreaks continued intermittently and with decreasing vigor until Pliocene and late Quaternary times.

Even more important than the Tertiary period of vulcanism was the alteration of the older topography by the slow upthrusting of the Sierra Nevada, the San Gabriel, the San Bernardino, and the San Jacinto Mountains, and the numerous ranges of the Great Basin area. The upheaval of these enormous blocks of the earth's crust was not a single cataclysmic event, sudden and violent, but a series of successive uplifts beginning in the late Tertiary and extending almost up to our times. The causes which initiated these crustal movements are not known, but the significance of the event is great, for as an inevitable consequence there came marked alterations of the climate and changes in the adjacent drainage systems. Many of the streams which formerly passed to the oceans were dislocated and forced to carry their sediments into undrained interior basins.

When first we visit the desert and see the present broad, flat-floored, sun-drenched basins,[1] the verdureless, sharp-crested mountains, and the dry streamways, it seems unnatural to picture it as ever a land with more humid climate and dotted with lakes. Yet all the evidence produced by the geologists points to the fact that such a land it was in times (Pleistocene) which succeeded the period of mountain building just mentioned. The accompanying maps, contrasting the present lake areas of the Great Basin with their abundance during recent geologic ages, show in unmistakable manner the climatic changes which have since taken place. In many places where now are dry gravel slopes or *bajadas* and arid, deep-set basins, running streams and bodies of living

---

[1] The term basin (not valley) is the appropriate one to use when speaking of the undrained mountain- or hill-rimmed depressions of the desert area. A valley is a *drained* trough-like depression with in-branching tributaries cut under the leadership of running water.

water then offered sanctuary to wild fowl and wading birds.
In regions at present so barren that only a few wild mice
can gain sustenance from the seeds borne by small, scrubby
plants, large mammals such as the mastodon, camel, and
ancient horse found a sufficiency of green food.

Lake Bonneville, fed to its fullness by streams derived
from the more plentiful rains and the melting glaciers of the

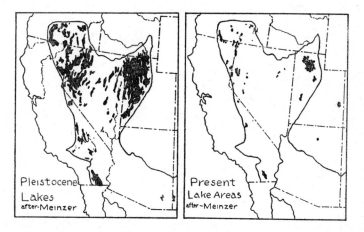

lofty Wasatch Range, once covered almost one-third of the
area of the present state of Utah. The basin of the former
Lake Lahontan (La-hon'-tan), occupying a series of con-
fluent depressions, principally in the western half of Nevada,
was filled by the mighty streams from the snow and glaciers
of the Sierra Nevada.

That there were many climatic oscillations in this time of
recent lake formation, that is, periods of drought interspersed
between long cycles of wet seasons, cannot be doubted by
those who see, about the margins of the old lake-basins, the

well-marked and beautifully preserved beach terraces and other shore features which indicate the different levels reached and maintained over considerable periods by the waters. The high-water stages indicated by the highest shore lines probably correspond to the different glacial epochs. In the Lahontan Basin there are records of three and perhaps four distinct lake stages. During the inter-glacial epochs, the basins were deserts much as they are today.

If we turn to the recent lacustrine history of the Mohave and Colorado deserts we have a most fascinating story with

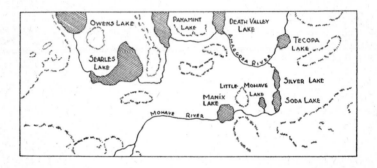

its scenes laid at our very doors. The author can suggest no more instructive and inspiring journey than a trip tracing the course of some of the ancient drainage channels and the sites of the placid lakes that once occupied our near desert basins.

To the east of the bold Sierra which form the backbone of California are four large, longitudinal, almost furrow-like depressions separated by parallel ranges of desolate, steep-pitched mountains. In each of these troughs there were basins which became at this time of more humid climate the

sites of ancient lakes. Streams derived from rains and melting Sierran glaciers provided the waters which formed these
lakes and linked them into a peculiar and well-defined series.

The first of the lakes to appear occupied a flat at the lower
end of Owens Valley. It was a deep body of fresh water
very much larger than the present shrunken salina, the white,
almost dry, salt-incrusted surface of which we now see
glistening like a blanket of snow on the desert floor. The
strands and gravel bars, marking by their levels the varying
depths of its waters and the climatic fluctuations of those
distant times, are plainly visible even to this day as we travel
along the motor highway skirting the western shores of
Owens Lake. The fact that they appear so fresh is convinc-
ing evidence that the lake cannot be so very old when compared to the much-worn mountains which rise in steep pitches
to the east and west of it. Overflowing its southern brink
during periods of high water, the lake sent a stream into the
broad, shallow basin known as Indian Wells Valley, thence
onward through Salt Wells Valley to Searles Basin. Here
another large lake was formed which at its highest stage not
only covered most of the Searles Basin but backed up through
Salt Wells Valley westward into Indian Wells Valley. A
good idea of its size may be gained by observing on the sides
of the encircling mountains the abandoned shore lines. These
stand out with remarkable clearness on the bold and rugged
Slate Range when viewed from the south side of the lake
just after sunrise. The highest of them shows that this body
of water once stood more than six hundred feet above the
floor of the present basin. A remarkable group of steep crags
made of calcareous tufa precipitated from the waters with
the aid of algae or bacteria are found at the southwest end

of Searles Lake. These spectacular rocks, often called the Pinnacles, rise about one hundred feet above the parched desert plain and remind one of the tall conical termite nests found in tropical Africa. They are scattered singly or in clusters over an area of several square miles, forming a major scenic attraction.

When Searles Lake was at its highest level its excess waters spilled from its southern end over into a low trough known as Pilot Knob Valley, and, after pursuing an eastward course, turned north and filled a basin in the deep Panamint

Trough. Here another great body of water over nine hundred feet deep and fully sixty miles long reflected from its mirrored surface the light from a more temperate sun. Brimming to its full capacity, Panamint Lake probably discharged through Wingate Pass into Death Valley, where the fourth of this chain of prehistoric lakes was established.

With the drying of the climate all of the lakes acted as concentration basins for the salts which had been leached out from the rocks and carried into them by inflowing streams. In the lowest parts of the basins, the saline deposits, mixed with alluvium carried down from the surrounding hills, formed conspicuous playas or mud flats. Some of them are surfaced with a smooth, hard floor of clay; most, however, are covered with rough, buffy-brown layers of dried mud. After heavy seasonal rains or after cloud-bursts the expansive flats are sometimes covered with water, but to a depth of only a few inches.

In Searles Lake is a deep-lying deposit of unusually pure salts, from sixty to one hundred feet thick, known as the crystal body. It is from this mineral storehouse that the American Potash and Chemical Company pumps the brines from which it recovers so many commercially valuable products. No such rich deposits have been found in Death Valley or Panamint Lake, but Owens Lake has yielded large amounts of valuable salines. The salts are found concentrated in the form of carbonates, sulphates, chlorides, and borates.

Just as the Owens River acted as the feeder for a series of lakes, so the Mohave River formed during this same humid period a chain of lakes along its course. The uplifting of the San Bernardino and San Gabriel Mountains in late Tertiary times provoked increased rainfall and greatly augmented previous drainage. It presumably better developed this stream which we now call the Mohave River. It must then have been a river of considerable size, for even in the arid climate of today it flows above ground or beneath the surface of the sands for one hundred and forty-five miles across the desert wastes. Freighted with gravels, sands, and clays, the reinforced river built up an enormous outwash plain, which stretched to the northward as far as the hills near the present site of Victorville. After wandering for a time back and forth over the surface of its flood plain, it finally established for itself a permanent course. But in wearing down its channel it met some hard rock masses (really tops of granite hills) which lay buried beneath the river bed; and, following the habit of rivers in such cases, it cut a channel through them. The small, but impressive gorge which was eroded constitutes the First Narrows of the Mohave just to the south of Victorville. The tracks of the Santa Fe Railroad now lie in the ancient cut. A little farther to the north the stream wore down a channel through a second group of similar rocks. A river acting as this one did is called by the geologists a superimposed river because the present stream channel was superimposed on the old granite hills. Both above and below the Narrows the river cut a channel in a broad flood plain of alluvium.

About forty miles east of Barstow it entered a depression rimmed on the east by the much-folded, -faulted, and -eroded Cave Mountain and Cady Mountain. The basin caused the river to expand into a shallow lake, which eventually covered an area of at least two hundred, and perhaps three hundred, square miles. The geologists refer to it as Lake Manix because a railroad station of that name lies in the midst of the old beds. Following a dry period when the area was converted into a playa, and a time of deposition of alluvial sediments, the lake reappeared. The accumulating waters at last found a point of egress at the basin's northeast end, and a channel was cut which finally became so deep that the lake was completely drained. The large gorge through which the stream poured is known as Cave Canyon. Passengers on the Union Pacific Railway may view its picturesquely eroded and highly colored walls as the train passes between Afton and Baxter, about forty-two miles east of Barstow. It is one of the great scenic attractions of the Mohave region. The Spanish priest, Fray Francisco Garces, in 1776 passed through this canyon on his way from the Mohave Indian villages on the Colorado River to the Mission San Gabriel. To the "arroyo of saltish waters" he gave the name Arroyo de los Martires.[2]

The greenish alluvium of the old Lake Manix beds may be observed at the head of Cave Gorge. In the canyon proper it is overlain by spectacular, red-buff conglomerates. Dr. Buwalda of the California Institute of Technology found in these Lake Manix clays fossil remains of a mastodon, an antelope, camels, horses, and a bird, all considered to be of Pleistocene age.

Emerging at the lower end of Cave Canyon, the Mohave River entered the upper reaches of a great north-south intermont trough which stretches with but minor interruptions to the lower end of Death Valley. It now began wandering

[2] The Mohave River Valley was the great roadway along which the early travelers passed into and out of southern California. The reasons are obvious: it furnished water for the human travelers and both food and water for their animals. Hither passed the American trapper, Jedediah Smith, also Kit Carson, Frémont, and Dr. Lyman. It was Frémont who gave the river its name. From him we have that old spelling, "Mohahve." The Old Spanish Trail followed eastward along the Mohave River as far as Soda Lake, where it turned northward along Silver Lake and Silurian Dry Lake to a spring of bitter waters called Salt Spring. Sometimes travelers broke away from the river route at a point a little to the east of the Calico Mountains and continued by way of Bitter Springs and along the east side of the Avawatz Range to Salt Springs. From this point of meeting, all travelers passed northward along the sandy wash of the Amargosa River until near the present site of Tecopa, where they turned eastward through Resting Springs and Stump Springs, climbed a pass in the south end of the scenic Spring Mountain Range, and then made their way to Vegas Spring.

in crooked ways over its outwash plain of detritus. The grade was so slight that at times the stream passed along a northward radius of its fan into Cronese Basin and established a shallow lake of sufficient permanence to encourage the growth of mollusks. The usual course of the river was then, as it is at present, eastward, and it finally entered Soda Lake, an enormous playa appropriately called the Sink of the Mohave. The volume of water which at times came down from the mountains must have been considerable, for, after filling Soda Lake Basin, now and then the river overflowed northward across an inbuilt dividing fan to Silver Lake Basin and at last to Death Valley, which, as indicated above, is but a natural extension of the trough. The Los Angeles–Salt Lake highway crosses Soda Lake at Baker Station, and the Death Valley road passes along the entire length of Silver Lake.

Death Valley received the final flow of still another ancient river, the Amargosa, or river of bitter waters, which arose then, as it does today, in one of the sequestered intermont troughs to the east of Death Valley. Though its catchment area was larger than that of the Mohave River and one of the most extensive in the Great Basin, the stream probably never discharged into the Death Valley Lake a large quantity of water. Death Valley Lake was so short-lived that presumably no well-cut terraces were ever formed about its rim.

In geologic times the Amargosa and the Mohave River united before they reached Death Valley. At the present time the salty Amargosa occasionally reaches Death Valley when heavy winter rains or cloudbursts augment the usual meager flow; but the Mohave River, even during the wettest seasons, never gets farther than Silver Lake and generally no farther than Soda Lake.

"Probably at some time at the end of the Tertiary period," says L. F. Noble, "the waters of the Amargosa River were ponded in Amargosa Valley and a lake was formed in which beds of clay, sand, and gravel were deposited. These deposits cover all the floor of the valley between Tecopa and a point north of Shoshone and extend several hundred feet up the slopes on the sides of the valley—their total thickness probably does not exceed 400 feet. These beds cover an area of at least 100 square miles, which indicates approximately the maximum extent of the lake. After the basin of the lake was filled with sediments, possibly to the level of its outlet, the Amargosa River began to cut down through the barrier to lower its beds. Since that time it has carved for itself, below Tecopa, a deep, rocky canyon which is one of the striking scenic features of the region. As the river bed was progressively deepened, the base-level of the Amargosa Valley above the barrier was lowered; and the lake deposits were subjected to erosion. As a result they have been dissected almost to their base, so that over most of the area in which they are exposed they now form mesas and bad lands."

This remarkable region of bad-land topography is all too often overlooked by the traveler as he passes northward toward Shoshone on the Silver Lake–Death Valley road.

At the head of the Gulf of California lies the Salton or Cahuilla Basin, a narrow depression, nearly three hundred miles long, set between the Peninsular Range on the southwest and the Little San Bernardino and Chocolate Mountains on the northeast. It forms the larger part of what we generally call the Colorado Desert, a name given because of its close proximity to the lower end of the Colorado River. Like the Mohave Desert, which borders it on the north and east, its most interesting recent geological history is bound up with lake formation and a river which ran into it.

Marine deposits discovered in the tilted rock beds at Painted Hill near Whitewater, also in similar formations near the mouth of Thousand Palms Canyon in the Indio Hills, in Carrizo Creek southwest of the Salton Sea, and at other places in the present Salton Basin, show that the sea in Miocene or Pliocene times, that is, long before the formation of the present Salton Trough, occupied much of the region, perhaps extending almost to the San Gorgonio Pass at Banning. The waters abounded with corals, huge oysters, and many other mollusks. Of greatest interest is the fact that many of these animals now found as fossils show affinity with kinds found in West Indian seas, suggesting that in those ancient times (enormously more ancient than those which marked the formation of Lake Manix and Death Valley Lake) there was interchange of waters between the Gulf of Mexico and the Pacific Ocean.

The recent studies of Drs. Buwalda and Stanton indicate that our old ideas concerning the Salton Sink's history must be recast. It was formerly held that, because its floor was below sea-level, the Salton Basin was occupied in recent times by a northward extension of the Gulf of California, and that the ancient Lake Cahuilla, or Blake Sea, which succeeded it, was but a portion of this arm of the Pacific Ocean cut off by a barrier of silt built up by the Colorado River.

It is now believed that the present deep, below-sea-level trough was produced by subsidence of the floor of the depression long, long after the last invasion of the sea. It is also believed that the building of the fan-like delta of the Colorado River was taking place while the land was still sinking. The delta, rising higher, growing wider, and finally reaching the western rim of the trough near the Cocopah Mountains, acted as a continuously increasing barrier against any possible new invasion of the sea. The wanderings of the silt-laden stream on the rapidly forming, almost dead-level delta were such that it discharged alternately into the Gulf and into the Salton Depression. This fluctuation of the stream's course probably occurred not once but many times. Whenever the Colorado flowed into the undrained basin, a lake quickly formed. On one of those recent occasions when the river changed its course back to the Gulf and discharged there for a long time, the lake to which it had given birth dried up and the desert again took possession.

With one or two exceptions not fully explained all of the little shells now found in the horizontal beds and sands of the Colorado Desert are mollusks which lived in these fresh-water lakes formed by the fickle river. The old water lines, strand formations, and crusts of travertine, so well seen near Coral Reef and at Travertine Rock, are not of marine origin, as is often thought, but are products of the fresh-water lakes formed by incursions of the Colorado River. It is well to note that the highest beach line which surrounds the Salton Basin is not at sea-level contour but lies somewhat above. Below are the ancient strands marking the various levels of the receding waters of the evaporating lakes. In many places concentric lines of sparsely growing plants serve as additional markers to show where the waters stood.

The present Salton Sea is about forty-seven miles in length and about seventeen miles in width at the widest point. The depth of the deepest portion averages about forty-five feet. Chemical analysis of the waters shows them to be quite like those of the open ocean. The Salton Basin in which the saline desert lake lies has an area of about 8,000 square miles, of which fully 2,200 are below sea-level. The lowest point is —273 feet.

CHAPTER III

PHYSIOGRAPHIC ASPECTS

OUR desert scenery is probably affected more by the presence of mountains than by any other geological feature. The monotony of the pale-faced basins is everywhere broken by the stern but colorful peaks and massive ridges which protrude island-like from the vast seas of sand and gravel. Some of the mountains rise abruptly from the desert floor; others ascend by long, smooth, concave slopes. Many, according to Wm. M. Davis, "have suffered so large a measure of erosion that their well-developed slopes have been worn back a mile or more, leaving an even rock floor or 'pediment,' veneered with thin patches of subangular gravel slanting gently forward to an intermont detrital plain." The bare rocky flanks are slashed by innumerable intricately enbranched gullies or shallow but often tortuous valleys. Extending from the mouths of the bowlder-strewn canyons are broad outwash fans consisting of a mixture of rocks, coarse gravels, sand, and silt which have been flushed from the mountain valleys. Coalescing, these outwash fans form broad alluvial aprons, which gradually slope downward

19

in beautiful sweeping curves to the centers of the basins. From a scenic standpoint I know of few features more appealing than these long, sloping fans when seen in profile. In the case of some of the older, much-eroded mountains, the fans reach almost to the crests and the worn-down cores appear to be buried in their own débris.

The powerful forces of deformation to which the earth was subjected in recent geological times produced in the Great Basin area great systems of intersecting or parallel crustal fractures. This desert province was thus broken into huge blocks and splinters, some of which, relatively or actually uplifted, more or less tilted, and carved down, formed our present mountains; while intervening blocks sinking or remaining at levels relatively lower formed troughs which since have been deeply filled with detritus from the worn-down mountains. The axes of these fault-block mountain ranges, like the major faults along which they arose, in general extend in a north and south direction. The Sierra Nevada and the ranges of the Death Valley area partake of this same northerly and southerly parallel arrangement, but the majority of the desert mountains to the southwest (i.e., in the mid-Mohave and eastern Colorado Desert), though associated with faulting,[1] seem to form no co-ordinated system, their major axes lying in almost every direction.

Among the many earth fissures of the desert area, the Garlock fault, located in the northern Mohave Desert, may be mentioned as an important example of one of our distinctly up-and-down mountain-making faults. This great crustal fracture begins near Tejon Pass, passes along the

---

[1] By faulting is meant the displacement of huge rock masses along fractures in the earth's crust.

southeast base of the Paso Mountains along the southern
border of Searles Basin to the lower end of the Slate Range,
and then eastward—a total length of two hundred miles!
Along much of its eastern part it is what we might call an
almost obliterated, worn-out fault; but along its middle and
western portion, motion has been so recent that one easily
sees breaks it has caused in the mountain scarps and in several of the alluvial fans it crosses.

The Death Valley and the Panamint faults appeal to our
interest because of the recent renewal of their activities and
because of the enormous escarpments or rock slopes that have
been formed along them on the east sides of their respective
"valleys." "When they are better known," says L. F. Noble,
"they will undoubtedly constitute one of the classic geologic
features of Western America." In the Panamint Trough
the escarpment, astonishingly fresh at its base, rises in a
remarkable, huge, sloping surface. The accompanying illustration shows the wide valleys which were eroded back

AFTER Wᵐ M. DAVIS

into an earlier uplifted scarp. It is evident that the mountains
thus carved were again uplifted carrying the valleys high up

on their slopes. The present drainage of these old valleys is through deep, ragged parallel slots cut in the surface of the newly exposed, almost smooth-faced rock slope below them. Small débris cones, recently built at the lower end of the slots, complete the picture of a goblet or wine-glass; hence the appropriateness of the term "goblet valleys" recently applied to them. The Panamint escarpment, seen to great advantage from the pass between Trona and Ballarat, is indeed one of the most impressive spectacles of that very remarkable region. One is well compensated for all the discomforts of motoring over the rocky roads to see it.

The San Andreas rift is probably the longest earth fissure of the North American continent: it is perhaps even longer than the enormous Rift Valley fault in the east of Africa. It may be taken as an example of a fault the complicated movements of which, mostly horizontal, are largely unrelated to mountain building. On the Mohave Desert this great linear earth fissure lies near the base of the San Gabriel Mountains. Continuing southeastward, after obliquely crossing a shoulder of this range, the master fault cuts the south base of the San Bernardino Mountains, then passes southeastward near the San Gorgonio Pass and along the northeast side of the Salton Basin, where it loses itself in the silts bordering the Salton Sea. "The group of mud volcanoes and solfataras at the lower end of the Salton Sea," says Walter C. Mendenhall, "may well be associated with a profound fracture of this nature."

Rivaling the work of mountain-building forces in changing the face of the land have been the forces of vulcanism. The wide dispersal of lavas and cinder cones in our desert regions bears testimony to the large-scale activity of vol-

canoes in the past. The black lava flows form a scenic feature that is appealing to every traveler. The unique form of
the cinder cones and their isolation in the broad basins or
atop the barren, chocolate-colored ranges is almost startling
when seen for the first time. The materials of which the
cones are composed are the cooled fragments of lava which
were thrown out from the vents, probably at the close of the
eruption. The fact that most of the cones are comparatively
low and broad indicates that the explosions were short-lived
but violent, probably lasting a few hours or at most a few

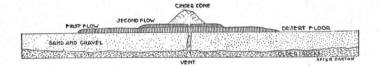

days. Throughout southwestern Utah (what perfect cones
there are near Yeyo!), across southern Nevada, and into
eastern and southeastern California there must be more than
a hundred of these cones, each showing some grace of line
or other feature of scenic charm.

Excellent views of lava flows and cinder cones of recent
origin (Pleistocene and later) may be had at Lavic, at
Amboy, in Owens Valley, and in the northern end of Death
Valley. A flock of twenty-seven cinder cones all huddled
together in a small area is visible from the state highway
between Baker and Halloran Spring. They lie directly to
the south near the Kelso Dunes. The Amboy cone, typical
of many others, is well described by Darton. He says: "In
the center of the basin, not far southwest of Amboy there
is a cinder cone on an extensive sheet of black lava (basalt).

This lava is geologically very recent and may have flowed out over the bottom of the basin within the last thousand years. It covers a nearly circular area about five miles in diameter. Its surface is remarkably rough, being covered with large blisters, most of them broken, and it has many caverns where the hot lava has run out at lower levels as it congealed at the surface. All the rock is black, practically unchanged by weathering, and full of vesicles or small holes, due to the escape of steam carried by the molten lava. The edge of the sheet is irregular, just as the lava congealed at the margin of the flow. The cone which is near the center of the flow is about two hundred feet high. It consists of a pile of black or dark-gray cinders or pumice, with a large crater at the center. In its southwest side there is a deep breach, from which extends a thin later sheet of lava that flowed over the main sheet."

A short distance beyond Newberry and to the south of Troy station is a cone remarkable because it is mounted high on the mountains. From its borders may be traced the course of the lava stream which flowed from its vent down a narrow valley almost to the level of the highway. As the traveler approaches the narrow-throated entrance to Owens Valley at Little Lake there is to the right a group of similarly high-mounted cones and he may see where the viscid lava on its descent down steep canyons plunged over precipices and congealed in the perfect likeness of waterfalls. One needs little imagination to picture the blowing cones and glowing red lava as it poured down the gorges in the blackness of a desert night.

From points along the crooked, one-track desert road which leads from Fenner north to Cima can be seen a most spectacular formation of deep-red volcanic rocks in which have been eroded an unusual number of large pocket-like recesses, caves, tunnels, shallow alcoves, and deep, slot-like gorges. Beyond are hills capped by erosion-resisting tabular malapais and several picturesque, flat-topped mesas or table mountains, really residual hills on which remain parts of the great lava sheet which once covered much of the desert country. These monuments of erosion are made up of colorful sheets of consolidated volcanic ash, separated by layers of light-colored lavas, and look "just like chocolate layer cakes," as a lad once said to me. The region is well worth a visit.

Black Mountain, northwest of Barstow, cloaked with black basic lavas, marks the center of another instructive volcanic field. The several drainage channels cut far back into the mountain mass afford a splendid opportunity to study the geologic history at first hand. Here in cross-section one can see at the base the tilted and eroded Tertiary strata upon which lie beds of consolidated ash and lava, and then on top a thin blanket of basalt. Many of the rocks exhibit remarkable examples of folding, tipping, and faulting.

In desert lands the sun, the winds, and violent rainstorms acting in conjunction with the forces of chemical decomposition are the great agencies which bring about the remarkable transformation in the landscape. All are at work scouring and shifting to bring the land to a country of flat, monotonous scenery. It is only because our deserts are, physiographically speaking, so very young that we have such varied topography, such variety of structural details.

It is always interesting to see how the different kinds of rocks have yielded to the labors of these erosive agents. By reason of the difference in their habits of disintegration and their behavior under stream and sheet-flood erosion, two classes of mountain-making rocks are distinguished—granitic and non-granitic. Just as the student of trees readily distinguishes, even at a distance, the different kinds by the form of their crowns, so the student of land forms learns to discriminate between mountains made of granitic and those made of non-granitic rocks by their surface texture and their general form. Mountains of granite when attacked by erosional forces retain their steep faces until reduced to mere heaps of bowlders. Non-granitic mountains, on the other hand, when wearing down, in most cases meet the detrital slopes of rock floors surrounding them in smooth concave curves, so that when seen from a distance they often assume a tent-like form.

In several places the erosional forces, working away for ages at the solid, uniform-structured granite mountains, have reduced them to large-scale, convex structures of low relief known as domes. One of the most beautiful of these is the

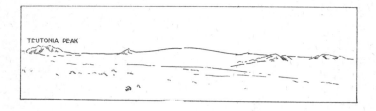

Cima dome (*cima* is Spanish for summit), seen to great advantage from the Barstow–Las Vegas highway near Valley Wells. A scenic road which begins east of Valley Wells

penetrates southward through a magnificent joshua-tree forest and leads the traveler near the broad, rounded summit and to several remarkably fine groups of rock nubbins and residual bowlders. Other similar and no less impressive features of granitic areas are the elongated domes known as arches. One of these, called the Cuddleback Arch and located about twenty-five miles northwest of Barstow, presents a spectacular, rounded crest which extends northwest–southeast for almost twenty miles. The even contour of the arch is broken by a number of scenic mounts; and near its northeast end is Pilot Knob, that great landmark of the mid-Mohave Desert.

In many places where the alluvium appears to be banked deep against mountainsides or over the ascending surfaces of domes and arches, it forms, as above described, but a thin cover for a low-angled slope or pediment of solid rock. A good example of such a rock floor covered with detritus occurs to the east of Silver Lake, where the smooth, gradual

slope has, except near the top, every appearance of being made of alluvium; yet only a few feet down is found a surface of solid granite. The upper reaches of these pediments may be robbed of their cover of detritus by sheet floods, and there is left only a barren rock surface ornamented here and there by small stones and isolated bowlders.

Dry lakes or playas, also sometimes called mud flats, occupy many of the undrained intermont basins or *bolsons* (Mexican word for "purses") of the Mohave and Colorado deserts. When seen from mountain elevations or airplanes they are striking features of the desert scenery. The mud-charged run-off from the bordering mountains, accumulating at the lowest point, forms ephemeral lakes, shallow but often extensive. Left to exhaustion by evaporation they soon become hard, brownish or gray, smooth-surfaced flats of clay (dry-type playa) or, if salts are present in quantity and the subsoil drainage is poor, they become pasty, wet-surfaced *salinas* (wet-type playa). "They correspond," says William Foshag, "to basins that are not water-tight and those that are, and this in turn determines their efficiency in retaining the salts brought into the basin."

Desert settlers find that wells sunk in the dry-type playas sometimes yield fresh water suitable for drinking but that waters derived from the wet-type playas are generally bitter with salts. The salt-incrusted flats often remain wet or moist at the surface during most of the year, or if any parts of the areas are dry they are covered with so-called self-rising soil, a dry, powdery, puffy soil into which the traveler sometimes sinks almost to his knees. Ordinarily the apparently dry surfaces are shallow; beneath is a stratum of slimy, tenacious mud full of salts.

Rosamond and Rogers lakes, also Silver Lake and Ivanpah Lake, are typical examples of large, dry-type playas; Searles Lake, Danby and Bristol dry lakes, and Soda Lake belong to the wet class. Let the driver of a motor car beware of these dry lakes in wet weather. I have myself experienced the perils of getting mired in the slippery mud and have seen cars which were abandoned because there was no hope of getting them out before the return of dry weather.

In nature nothing is more constant than change. Just as the mountain surfaces are continually being altered by erosion, so the seemingly permanent rocks of which they are composed are breaking down under the forces of chemical decay (oxidation, hydration, carbonation, and solution) and disintegration ("physical disruption of rocks to form particles of smaller size").

Many of the rocks, though seemingly very hard, are really quite quickly worn away by running or falling sediment-bearing water. Along the deeply incised courses of the intermittent mountain streams, large pockets are hollowed out beneath the temporary cascades attending cloudburst freshets. These natural rock basins, filled with coarse gravels and sand from the torrential waters, are known as tanks or *tinajas*. They retain in the gravel interstices the purest, sweetest drinking-water known to the desert traveler. Animals, such as the bighorn sheep and the ever-wise coyotes and donkeys, as well as prospectors, possess knowledge of the presence and freshness of these reservoirs and how the waters may be tapped by digging holes and trenches in the coarse sands. Even the insects are aware of the location of these "coyote" wells, as they are often called, and several times when in need of water I have located such places by watching converging lines of thirsty bees.

It is the hard granite and nearly related rocks encircling the desert basins which furnish most of the material from which the great sand dunes are made. The sands of the

Devil's Playground and of the billowy dunes near Kelso are probably derived from the Granite Mountains and adjacent granitic outcrops along the Mohave River to the west.

The dunes east of Kelso and near Soda Lake, while not the most extensive, are perhaps the highest and most spectacular on the California deserts. From great distances their pure sands may be seen gleaming in the brilliant sunshine. Passengers on the Union Pacific Railroad are fortunate in passing so near them that in spring they may see the undulating surfaces carpeted with sweet-odored primroses, verbenas, and golden garaeas.

The impressive and stupendous Algodones Dunes of the Colorado Desert, crossed by the highway between Brawley and Yuma, form a nearly continuous belt five to seven miles wide and almost fifty miles long, reaching from Mammoth Station to a point below the California-Mexico boundary-line near Yuma. They are made up of sands derived not only from the disintegration of the rocks of the mountains bounding the great Salton Depression but also from the breakdown of the yellowish sandstones of the old Tertiary marine beds. Just how old these dunes are no one knows; they are probably of considerable age. Their extreme narrowness and great length present several problems not easy to solve. It is possible that their original windward slope was trimmed back by wave action at a time when the water level of the Salton Sea stood much higher than it does at present.

Persons traveling to Palm Springs will do well to stop and examine the small dunes found near the Snow Creek bridge. From their peculiar form they are known as elephant-head dunes. The windward surfaces are covered with luxuriant growths of that efficient sand-catching plant, the ever-verdant ephedra, or desert tea; the lee sides of many of the sand humps are barren, but from them often protrude strange proboscis-like ridges.

Important accumulations of dune sand are found also at the north end of the Maria Mountains, both at the north and at the south end of Death Valley, along the lower Amargosa River, in the Mohave River Valley northwest of Newberry, near Roger's Dry Lake, around Cadiz Dry Lake, and northwest of Twenty-nine Palms. A few barchanes or traveling crescentic dunes are found about four miles north of Kane Spring near the margin of the Salton Sea.

Heaps of dune sand are generally related either to old lake beaches or to permanent eddies in the wind system. As an illustration of those related to beaches, the old dunes north of Roger's playa in the Mohave Desert may be mentioned. The beautiful group of dunes at the north end of Death Valley and the large dunes east of Palm Springs Station on the Colorado Desert illustrate those due to peculiarities of the wind-currents.

Any land area dominated by dunes should be often visited if for no other reason than to study light effects and glorious colors. Every hour of the day marks changes, and morning or evening the clean sands, viewed from a distance, are marvelously rich in diaphanous shades of purple, pink, blue, and yellow. Partly clouded, moonlit skies add to the effect, and under the clearing skies following rains every dune is a changing panorama of glory. Winter days near Kelso and Crucero on the Mohave Desert, at Palm Springs, and at Glamis on the Colorado Desert are never to be forgotten!

Sands, picked up and drifted along at times of severe wind storms, become one of the desert's very strongest agents of abrasion. They etch away every object with which they come in contact, not excepting the traveler's cheek and the enamel of his automobile. Nowhere is this filing action of sand in motion better exhibited than along the dry streamways of the Whitewater River on the Colorado Desert or in the lower end of Death Valley. Natural sandblasts cut the bark from all the living shrubs which have been so unfortunate as to take root there. Filing away at the rocks, they carve out the softer portions and leave the more resistant parts protruding in miniature, dike-like ridges and pinnacles.

The country to the south and west of the Salton Sea is a region dominated by bold, bare mountain forms and waterless sand and clay plains, over the surface of which are distributed innumerable, odd-shaped, banded rocks which pique the curiosity of modern travelers even as they did the ancient Indians, who regarded the region as the abode of evil spirits. These rocks seem to be imitations cut in stone of every beast known and every grotesque god conceived of by ancient man. Many of them have taken on the forms of vegetables, and we often hear of fossil cabbages, turnips, and kelps brought in by the curious hunters of souvenirs who with pride pile them up in their home gardens or place them in mineral cabinets to excite the curiosity of their neighbors. The common explanation is that they are due to weathering of the iron-stained sandstones, but geologists who have studied them with care have not satisfactorily accounted for their formation.

In many of the brown, vegetationless, mud hills of the

Carrizo region numerous plates of weathered gypsum lie exposed, many of them as flat as windowpanes and as large as dinner plates. From a considerable distance their smooth surfaces may be seen reflecting the sunlight, thus adding a peculiar weirdness to the landscape. The eroded hills have taken on queer rounded forms and some of them are highly colored. The dried mud on the surface is curiously puffed owing to the development of salt crystals which, on forming after rains, heaved the clay surface upward. Similar barren, crumpled, clay hills, full of salt and gypsum, are features of the landscape near Saratoga Springs in southern Death Valley.

Desert mosaic, so-called desert pavement, is of common occurrence in the areas of igneous or volcanic rocks, though not entirely confined to these regions; limestone tracts have it too. Often over wide areas, acres in extent, the ground surface appears to have been paved with countless pebbles or small stones and rolled down to flatness with a steam roller. Perhaps a creosote bush here and there is all there is to break the wide monotony of the clear, tessellated rock-floor. Both wind and rain are the responsible agents. An examination of the myriads of little flat stones will reveal that they have settled on a bed of fine alluvium with the longest axis parallel to the ground surface, the position easiest taken when settling to rest after beating rains or winds loosen or agitate the fine soil beneath them. These pavements make pedestrian travel difficult in summer, because of the hard, smooth surface, and also because of the glaring light reflected from the "varnished" rocks.

This "desert glaze" or "varnish," which makes the rocks appear coated with oil, is common not only on pavement pebbles but also on many of the larger rock-surfaces in all arid countries. It has long been thought to be solely due to the slow deposition of certain soluble constituents which have been drawn to the surface of the rocks by the sun's rays. But it has recently been shown that lichens growing on rocks having a manganese and iron content may also be active agents in the formation of desert varnish. (See page 161.)

In masses of conglomerate rocks found on the desert slope of the San Gabriel Mountains and considered to have been formed in Eocene times are imbedded rocks with brown and black coatings of desert varnish, showing that arid conditions favorable to the deposition of desert varnish existed even in those ancient times.

CHAPTER IV

WEATHER AND CLIMATIC FEATURES

IF WE are so fortunate as to visit our deserts during several successive seasons or over a period of years we soon discover that there is a well-defined desert climate, with four seasons climatologically as well as biologically well marked. The transition from one season to another in these semi-tropical deserts is usually gradual, much more so than in deserts farther to the north and more inland. Nowhere do we see here the abruptness of seasonal changes so characteristic of the Gobi and other deserts of central Asia.

It is largely due to winds that deserts are made (see page 2), and winds constitute one of the desert's most interesting weather phenomena. On our California deserts the summer winds, though warm, are usually moderate, but in winter and spring the air-currents push with much vigor. Winds from the northeast, known as "Santa Anas" when they reach the southern Californian coast, are the worst, and at times reach velocities of forty miles or more an hour. They often come on with extraordinary abruptness following rainstorms; being very dry, they dissipate the moisture-bearing clouds in a short time.[1] Their maximum strength is attained soon after sunrise. Picking up fine particles of soil on dry lake basins and dunes, they fill the atmosphere with dust clouds, furiously lash the vegetation, and set every insecure thing on the move. These are the winds that cause prospectors to put all sorts of curious braces on their shanties and to nail doubly the sideboards and shingles. If they are caught while camping out, they must weigh down with rocks everything from tarpaulins to dishpans. The wind usually drops at sunset and the nights are then surprisingly calm: the red skies of sunset change to clear blue-black and sparkle with myriads of brilliant stars. The smoke of the campfire now ascends "straight up."

Recently I had on the deserts of western Nevada an unnerving experience with the winds that left on my mind an image so deeply etched that it can never be effaced. It was in the month of March. All day I had labored against a strong southwest wind that was prophetic of soaking rains. Sure enough, before night the precipitation came, but it was in the form of snow. I found shelter in a miner's cabin, put a pot of beans on the stove to cook, and went to bed, expecting at daybreak to waken and find myself snowed in for at least one or two days. With a suddenness that was startling, the wind at nine o'clock veered squarely to the north and began blowing with a hurricane violence that set every timber in the little shanty creaking and groaning. Though the

---

[1] The air of the Santa Anas is warmed by compressional heating and becomes very dry. Since the air currents are descending, turbulence or vertical convection, so essential to cloud formation, ceases.

house was well braced it seemed every minute that it must go. There was nothing to do but wait under cover, for it would have been little better than suicide to venture out of doors. The eerie effect was heightened by the continuous, thunderous roar, while the angry wind continued unabated until near daybreak.

Violent north winds are usually of only a few days' duration. The strong winds that blow with most protracted violence are those which come in from the Pacific Coast, hailing the approach of winter rains. Nimbus clouds and lenticular clouds, appearing like great Zeppelins over the western mountains, are heralds of their oncoming. The clouds continue beating their way in, often seemingly against odds, until at length they cover the skies. Then silence comes and the rain descends, at first gently, but steadily increasing to a downpour. The stronger the initial winds, the better the chances for precipitation.

During the months of April and May, when fog is commonest on the Coast, the period of violent sand-and-dust storms comes to the upper Colorado Desert, especially in the San Gorgonio Pass[2] and along the course of the White-

---

[2] Few people recognize what a great draught channel the San Gorgonio Pass is. As W. P. Blake long ago pointed out, through it the air pours "from the ocean to the interior with peculiar uniformity and persistence, thus supplying the partial vacuum caused by the ascent of heated air from the surface of the parched plains and deserts." The wind "is not an ordinary shifting breeze, but is a constant, powerful current of air sweeping through the pass from the west. It pours from the Pacific in an apparently unbroken, unvarying stream, passing over the surface with such violence that all the fine grains of sand are lifted from the dry channels of the streams and are driven along the descending slopes until they find a final resting-place to the leeward of the projecting spurs" of San Jacinto.

water River to the Salton Sea. It is these winds sweeping in from the Coast that, picking up the sands, and often pebbles as large as peas, etch the windshields and painted surfaces of motor cars, blind the traveler's eyes with dust, and cause him so many unhappy hours. It is wise to avoid desert travel when the coastal fogs of spring are on. But there is always something deeply and highly exciting and weird in the sounds of these storms, particularly in the singing of the wind-driven sands, and I have many times purposely pushed out on foot into them to hear the wild music.

A wind known as the "evening blow" is common in summer. It is probably a local adjustment phenomenon. It arises about sundown and is a strong, steady west wind that does much to drive out the heated air of the long days and temper the weather for those who must live continuously in the interior regions. The average velocity is not great, about twenty miles an hour. It may continue well through the night but always drops before sunrise. It is best observed in long, trough-like depressions such as the Salton Sink, although the Mohavean mesas and interior basins get their share too.

Whirlwinds or tornillos are commonest on calm summer and autumn afternoons when all the air is shimmering with heat. They are due to the local heating of the air above the flat desert floor. During this period of seasonal calms there is generally at midday a lack of wind velocity sufficient to act as an impetus for any heat adjustment of the ordinary kind, and so it has to take place in the form of "explosions" or "leaks." As a result, swiftly rising columns of expanding air are formed. Currents of surface air move in to replace the air which is rising, and a whirl is developed. Gathering up sand and dust and bits of dried vegetation, the dust devil, as it is sometimes called, now begins to move slowly across the land, gathering momentum and gaining in height as it goes forward. Sometimes half a dozen or more of these wandering dust whirls, some of them a thousand feet high, are seen at one time. Watched from mountain tops, the slender chimneys of ascending dust are imposing and fascinating sights. On our southern California deserts they seldom assume destructive proportions, but in some of the broad Old World deserts they develop into violent storms.

The desert rains of the autumn, winter, and spring season are of the Pacific marine type. They come for the most part from the west and southwest. Energetic storms with high fronts then climb the Sierra and other coastal mountains, reaching not only the immediate desert, but far out across the Great Basin states of Nevada and Utah. Drenching rains of this type may occur as early as mid-October but are seldom experienced later than the first of April. The winter maximum of the Pacific Coast area asserts itself all over southern California and the interior deserts in January and February. The winter and spring quota of rainfall, where local conditions such as the altitude of mountain ranges do not increase it, progressively diminishes northeastward from the desert's western edge.

One of the pleasantest times to visit the desert is during periods when winter rains occur. Indeed, incoming rain clouds are generally for me the signal to start desertward. Let me have the delicious odors of the creosote bush and the salt bush when they are wetted with gentle rains, look upon the endless variety and beauty of the clouds' far-flung forms, have the silence of the uninhabited mesas, and I am in a land enchanted.

The higher mountains are often whitened by midwinter snows; some of them, such as Telescope Peak in the Panamint Mountains and Charleston Peak in the Spring Mountains of southwestern Nevada, may receive generous amounts and carry snow patches until midsummer. Most of the other ranges receive only temporary coverings, which last for from a few days to several weeks. One of the most fascinating sights of winter is the entire Mohave Desert blanketed with snow. At such times the individualization and varied configuration of the lost ranges are brought out in a way that is very marked. As you view these whitened highlands you feel indeed that you are in a new land of mystery, for "the tent-like mountains gleam like the encampment of some mighty host." On the high Mohave Desert, one may reasonably expect to experience a light fall of snow any time after the middle of November and as late as mid-April.

Not much is known concerning the humidity of desert areas. In general it may be said that in the open desert there is a large relative fluctuation. It is low at midday and relatively high at night, the greatest and most rapid alternations occurring in summer. It must always be kept in mind that the desert is very much the domain of sun and wind. Rain and snow are among its most infrequent phenomena. Day after day the sun beats down upon the barren soil, and the drying winds are seldom idle. All places get rain at some time, but hundreds of days often pass without a drop of it.

The summer rains of the desert are of the Gulf type. Water vapor is borne from the Gulf of California by southerly winds. Clouds soon form and bank up high over the heated interior basins. Much of this summer rainfall is spotted. It occurs on hot, quiet days and consists of cloudbursts, or heavy showers of short duration. These rains are generally for the moment accompanied by high, gusty winds carrying great clouds of dust. Precipitation may be of two or more inches in a short half-hour, producing what are known as sheet-floods. The waters gather together in the "oueds" or dry drainage channels, and on their onward march become freighted with sand, bowlders, and loosened trees and shrubs, which they carry down to the lower levels with a roar that may be audible, at least in the hush following the storm, for miles around. Woe to the foolish camper who has made his temporary home on the sands of the washes down which the waters rush! Pots, pans, and all his belongings, including his motor car, may be caught up in the swirling floods and come to a sad end.

The waters from these heavy rains run off so quickly that most of the desert vegetation profits little from them. Only the plants which live in the washes get a chance for a real drink. Among the curiosities encountered by the desert traveler are the local bits of verdure marking the courses of streamways which carry the flood waters. On the whole these torrents are very destructive to both plants and animals. Mice and other small burrowing animals are the greatest sufferers.

The hottest days of summer occur when low-pressure areas move in from the Coast and form immediately over the Great Basin. Then not only do desert dwellers swelter in the torrid heat[3] but also the inhabitants of the cities of the coastal strip. It must not be inferred that days of unfavorably high temperatures are far greater in number on the desert than at many points on the coastal side of the mountains. Cool days of summer on the Coast are matched by tolerably pleasant, though not as cool, weather on the desert. This is especially true of the Mohave Desert. Travelers will find it well to keep this in mind when beginning summer journeys involving desert travel in the daytime. It is really surprising how many days are agreeable and during how many nights a blanket is required for sleeping comfort.

The Colorado Desert owes much of its winter climatic excellence to its lack of snow and to the clear skies, ideal temperatures, and highly invigorating daily changes. The midday sun is delightfully warm and the night temperatures seldom bring frost. Winter days on the Mohave Desert are often equally pleasant and stimulating, but owing to the higher altitudes the nights are much cooler and over much of the region chilly temperatures and hard frosts are the rule. David G. Thompson records the average length of the growing season for crop plants at ten chosen stations on the Mohave Desert as 257 days. The average length of the growing season for cultivated crops at Indio in the Salton Sink may be placed at almost 365 days. The Colorado Desert's record for warm winter days is matched on the Mohave Desert only at Bagdad.

Considerable daily range in temperature is experienced in the climate of all great deserts, but it is well to remember

[3] Summer shade temperatures of 105° to 118° F. are frequent. The highest recorded shade temperature, 134° F., is from Death Valley.

that our Western North American deserts, because of their proximity to the regulating waters of the sea, are not subject to the daily extremes of heat and cold encountered in the interior of the great Palearctic deserts of Africa and Asia, where temperature ranges as great as 68° F. (from 31° to 99° F.) have been known within twenty-four hours. David G. Thompson, speaking of this temperature fluctuation on the Mohave Desert, says: "In summer the temperature frequently falls from above 100° in the daytime to below 75° or 70° at night, and in winter it frequently rises from below the freezing-point in the early morning to 65° or 70° at midday. The daily range is probably a little less in winter than in summer."

The intensity of aridity in desert lands is perhaps best expressed by what is known as the evaporation-rainfall ratio. It is the ratio between possible evaporation and actual rainfall, and it shows the discrepancy between the water upon which plants can draw and the desiccating effect of the desert climate and sun.

"It is," says Buxton, "of very great interest to biologists, and it is probably one of the most important factors in determining whether a place will or will not be desert. So far as we know it is high in all desert regions, and it is not high in regions which are not desert. In an unusually dry year the evaporation-rainfall ratio will be vastly increased, so that, at a time when the mere drought is pressing hardly on flora and fauna, an increased discrepancy between rainfall and evaporation is thrown into the scale against them."[4]

[4] Patrick Alfred Buxton, *Animal Life in Deserts: The Fauna with Relation to the Environment.* Edward Arnold & Company, London, 1923.

Observations to determine the possible evaporation have been made at several points in the American and in the Pale-arctic deserts. Pans and tanks of water were placed where they got the full play of sun and wind. The annual evaporation of Harold Reservoir (Mohave Desert) was found to be about 87 inches, that at Pahrump about 85 inches, that at Yuma about 100 inches, that at Tucson, Arizona, about 90 inches, and that at Cahuilla about 116 inches. In some parts of the Libyan Desert, where rain falls only once in every four or five years, the total of possible evaporation is believed to be close to 150 inches.

CHAPTER V

INSECTS AND THEIR NEAR RELATIVES

THE number of species of insects in any region as large as the one under consideration is so great that only a few of those most conspicuous in form and most interesting in their habits can be considered. As the specialized biology of these arid-region insects is unraveled they become more and more fascinating creatures for investigation. I find that their collection and study is one of the greatest sources of travel delight.

The most interesting question is concerned with the manner in which the desert insects manage to pull themselves through the times of summer heat and dryness or the long, protracted droughts when, for several seasons or even years, there is little or no food available for either larvae or adults. The question has recently been answered for the butterflies and moths, and it is quite possible that the way to a similar answer has been pointed out for most of the other insect groups. It is now known that when inimical conditions press hard upon the larval butterflies and moths they stop feeding and go into a kind of summer sleep, called aestivation, hiding the while under leaves and stones. There they lie in dormancy perhaps for months or years, until a fortunate season arrives. Then, immediately alert to the favorable conditions, they resume their normal life history. When in the pupal state they may again go into a long period of rest, some of them "holding over" two years or more before emerging.

Dr. P. A. Buxton has divided insects into two types, the "spenders" and the "savers," with a series of intermediates. The "spenders" he designates as those of damp climates which eat food of high water-content. They practice no economy of water but pass it freely in their excreta and feces and possibly through the body wall as well. To the second group belong the majority of insects living on deserts. Their food is dry and many of them withstand long starvation, living for months in parched sand without food or drink. Several kinds of water economy are practiced by these "savers." Some are almost proof against loss of water from the body surfaces; they excrete their uric acid in a solid state and extract water from the contents of the hind gut so that the feces pass dry. Others, subject to loss of water through evaporation, burn fat at a rate sufficient to replace it.

When burning heat kills the adult insects, their eggs may be the means of continuing the life of the species. These eggs, like the seeds of many plants, tolerating great dryness and in some cases the actual loss of water by the embryo itself, hatch only when moistened by the rains which end the dry spells. Eggs of springtails, normally hatching in 8 or 10 days, have been known, when dried, to live 271 days without dying. Eggs of one of the South African locusts, which in moist soils hatch in 14 days in summer, may remain alive in very dry soil for more than three years.

Under rocks and among dry sticks and leaves, the color of which they resemble to a remarkable degree, live those primitive, mottled-gray insects, the fishmoths or bristletails (*Thysanura*). They seem to mind neither the oven-like air nor the dryness, but they avoid the direct sunlight. These insects have protrusible vesicles on the abdominal segments and it has been suggested that these serve for absorption of water and therefore that the insects can take advantage of dew or other moisture when it is available.

The great order *Orthoptera,* which includes grasshoppers, crickets, walking-sticks, and katydids, is well represented by numbers of specialized forms. Dr. Morgan Hebard brings out the interesting fact that many of the desert grasshoppers have habits so individual that once we know these habits in connection with the exact locality where the insects live we may proceed at once to an identification without further aid. Specimens from one locality may look very much like those from another and still be widely different in habits. Bruner's silver-spotted grasshopper (*Bootettix argentatus*), with wings a rich green, spotted with brown and mother-of-pearl, is one of the handsomest insects of the desert. It lives exclusively on the creosote bush, never resting on the ground. If driven out it flies immediately to another creosote bush. It is certainly a good example of a creature of restricted habitat. In the month of June I have found the young, pale-green, wingless forms lined up by thousands on the slender, gray, woody stems. The ghostly grayish grasshopper that flies in undulations before you in Death Valley is *Anconia integra,* but in that region it is much more pallid than elsewhere. In late April and May, grasshoppers are not infrequently very plentiful on the Mohave Desert. They fly up in crackling clouds before the automobile sauntering along the winding desert roads. By hundreds they jump into the driver's seat and make such a rattling noise as they strike the windshield and the sides of the car that one may easily imagine he is in a hailstorm.

In Imperial Valley and about Yuma the Mexican ground cricket (*Nemobius mexicanus*) becomes a veritable pest in summer. Its persistent, pulsating chirp is one of the most familiar night sounds of that part of the desert. These crickets get into houses and eat clothing and are continually being trampled under foot. On several occasions strong winds have been known to carry swarms of them far to the northeastward into the higher desert valleys. The little native vegetation that was green was entirely consumed by their greedy jaws.

Very curious are the queer, earthen shelter-galleries built over dead desert shrubs by the Arizona desert termite (*Amitermes arizonensis*). Often the interior wood is almost entirely eaten away, leaving the fragile, earthen tubes to crumble to dust upon being touched. The insects are most active after summer rains, and at such times almost all of the dead shrubs over wide areas may appear like plants "spattered thick with mud." Four other species of "desert termites" (*Amitermes*) are found living in the bases of agaves, and in the trunks of desert willow, iron-wood, cholla, and ocotillo, but these build no extensive mud-tubes. The black-legged termite (*Reticulotermes tibialis*) occurs along the western border of the Colorado and Mohave deserts under stones and dead logs, in dead wood and cow-chips. The fact that the body of this insect is wholly black illustrates the folly of calling all termites "white ants." One interesting point about termites is the fact that almost all the species have, in their intestinal tract, thousands of tiny, one-celled parasites, known as flagellate protozoans. On these they depend for the digestion of the cellulose of the dry wood they eat. The protozoans are equally dependent upon their termite hosts. This interdependence is generally so marked that the termites die if freed of the protozoans and the protozoans die if deprived of their wood diet. It has been shown that the desert termites of the genus *Amitermes* are different from all other termite relatives, for they seem to get on perfectly well without their protozoan helpers! Just why, no one seems to know.

Strong of wing, the keen-eyed dragon flies make their way far from the water holes where their eggs are laid and the nymphs develop. It seems almost an anomaly that these insects, which we always associate with water, should at times hunt their insect prey twenty or perhaps thirty miles from the nearest known springs or streams, but seeing them do so is an experience frequent enough on deserts.

In the fine sands, and in the powdery soils that floor the shallow caves, we regularly see the queer, conical pits made by ant-lion larvae to snare their prey. The desert's ant population is so considerable that the rapacious larvae of these insects always find plenty to eat. The gray-winged adult ant lions are among the most persistent of the insects that collect about lights on a summer evening. The family to which these insects belong is particularly well represented in arid regions of many parts of the world.

The most remarkable scale insect of the desert area appears to be the creosote-bush lac-scale (*Tachardiella larreae*). For many of the scales, high temperatures and marked dryness are the greatest deterrents to existence. But here is one that not only tolerates heat but thrives on it.[1] The lac insects, crowded on the stems of the creosote bush, hide beneath warty coverings of dirty-brown or reddish resinous material. This resin was once valuable to the Indians, who used it as a mending material for their vessels. The oak wax scale (*Cerococcus quercus*) lives on the scrub oaks of the desert mountains; its waxy coverings are bright yellow and give a curious warty appearance to the branches bearing the closely crowded insects. I once heard that the Indians used this wax for chewing-gum, and out of curiosity I tried the golden sweetmeat, but found the nasty paste dreadfully bitter, indeed as unpalatable as wormwood. It is probable that had I persisted the end-product might have been better, but I did not then have, nor have I now, the courage to stay with the ordeal to its possible pleasant end.

The true bugs live on plant juices or on the blood of animals. The period of activity of these insects must in most cases necessarily coincide with the period of active plant growth. Following the advent of spring flowers they are seen everywhere and may continue to be found late in summer if any of the plants such as the wild buckwheats (*Eriogonum*) continue to grow. An examination of the tree yuccas in late March and early April will reveal enormous numbers

---

[1] Another coccid remarkably adapted to aridity is *Margarodes vitium,* which occurs in arid parts of South America. At the end of larval growth it becomes completely covered with a waxy coating and is then known as the "ground pearl." In this condition it can resist prolonged drying. When the cyst is put into damp soil it absorbs moisture and continues its development. Professor G. F. Ferris of Stanford University describes finding one of these sand pearls alive after seventeen years in a museum case!

of the prettily marked lateral leaf hopper (*Oncometopius lateralis*) swarming over the leaves. They hang on so tight that it is necessary to shake the branches vigorously to get them off.

In summer large broods of the apache cicada (*Diceroprocta apache*) appear in the Salton Basin and all through the day one hears their continuous *zing*. Often the mad chorus continues long after sunset. All during the sunny hours, while the cicadas are busiest singing, the great cicada killer (*Sphecius convallis*), a robust brown and yellow banded wasp, is fiendishly at work bringing in cicadas as her victims to provide food for her larvae. The paralyzed insects are stored in burrows made in the soil and on them the eggs of the wasp are laid.

Bold asilid or robber flies are frequently seen resting on the ground or darting about while carrying away, like hawks, their insect victims. A great, brown, hairy species of robust form, *Rhapionidas xanthos,* should be looked for emerging from sands and gravels in the high desert valleys in May. It belongs to a family of flies, species of which are very rare, though widely distributed in both hemispheres. The commonest desert asilid is a large gray species belonging to the genus *Erax.*

Various biting midges (*Chironomidae*) from salt and brackish waters of deserts are known throughout the world. These are the little black flies (e.g., *Leptonops kerteszi* var. *americanus*) that swarm so persistently about one's face on stuffy, warm evenings. They are exceptionally annoying on account of their fierce bites. They should not be confused with *Hippaletes flaviceps,* the salute fly so annoying in the Coachella Valley, which, after years of search, was found to pupate and to breed in decaying vegetation. Ephydrid or salt-marsh flies (*Ephydra hians* and *E. subopaca*) are found almost everywhere about salt and alkaline streams and lakes. The waters of Owens Lake and the brackish pools in Death Valley and the Salton Sink are teeming with the larvae. These, each about 12 mm. long, wiggle about in the almost syrupy briny or brackish waters and exhibit their remarkable anal breathing-tubes and their curious hooked legs, by means of which they often attach themselves to the bottom rocks. The Piute Indians are said to have collected and dried these larvae for food. That any living creature should be able to find a favorable environment in the concentrated salt waters is most remarkable. Pupation takes place beneath the water. The adults escape from the pupal case and are carried to the surface in a bubble of air. In these same brackish pools may sometimes be found the larvae of the great buzzing horse-fly (*Tabanus punctifer*), soldier flies (*Stratiomyidae*), water boatmen (*Corixidae*), and several small hydrophilid beetles whose life histories are imperfectly known.

As a rule, desert areas in the natural state are quite free from mosquitoes, but with the introduction of irrigation and the creation of many permanent and transient pools where their larvae may feed, mosquitoes become increasingly abundant. Twenty years ago when camping widely over the Salton Basin my night's sleep was seldom menaced by a mosquito, but now almost anywhere in the Valley a good night's rest in the open is impossible, even during the middle of the winter months. The Mohave Desert is as a whole still sufficiently dry to insure freedom from mosquito bites in most situations. The mosquito prevailing throughout the Imperial Valley is *Culex quinquefasciatus,* a common house mosquito of tropical and sub-tropical countries of the world. It breeds throughout the year in water holes, particularly polluted ones, wayside pools, and ditches. Winds often carry the adults far from their breeding-places, and this fact probably accounts for their wide distribution in waterless areas. *Anopheles pseudopunctipennis,* a malarial mosquito, is known to breed in roadside ditches near Thermal but is not here believed to be a carrier of disease. The larvae of *Theobaldia inornata* have been collected in the waters of many pools of the desert area. The adults, large mosquitoes with a persistent, low hum, often gather in disconcerting numbers about the camp at night.

Those specialized mosquitoes of the genus *Psorophora,* frequent enough in northern Mexico, may yet be found with us, since they are peculiarly adapted to desert conditions. The eggs, protected by tough spiny coats, are deposited singly in the bottoms of rain pools and may lie dormant for months or years awaiting their immersion in some transient pond formed by the infrequent rains. Upon hatching, the wrigglers pass through their life history in a very few days. The adults emerge as metallic insects of spidery appearance and vicious bite.

The coleoptera or beetles are among the most conspicuous of insects. Of these the darkling beetles of the genus *Eleodes* are particularly successful inhabitants of deserts, in both the Old World and the New. Contrary to the general law of desert animal coloration, the many species of *Eleodes* have bodies colored for the most part a deep black. This makes them very conspicuous and, in addition, subject to the maximum of heat absorption. Not only have they the sun beating down upon them but also they get the full effect of reflection from the hot earth beneath them. We probably have little appreciation of what high temperatures exist right down next to the ground-surface where they crawl. The amazing thing is that we often find them active during the hottest parts of the day as well as in the cooler hours of the night. Dr. Buxton has shown that these beetles may obtain a considerable amount of water by eating fragments of organic matter which have absorbed water from the atmosphere in the evening when dew is forming. He has also shown that such insects can keep their temperature slightly lower than that of their environment, presumably by evaporating water during the daytime. These beetles, known to the traveler as circus bugs because of the singular habit of standing on their heads with the tip of the abdomen thrust upward, are vegetarians, and often they visit the nests of harvester ants to feed on the fragmental remains of seeds and flowers which lie about the ant hills. In spring and early summer, which is their period of migration, they are found in great numbers.

The boring beetles (*Buprestridae*) and their larvae play a major part in reducing the dying vegetation to powder, and here perform the work done by the bacteria of more humid countries. Once wood is dead, it rapidly goes to pieces under their labors. Some of their activities are mentioned in connection with the desert trees (see pages 183, 184, 187, 191).

The wealth of unusual species and the abundance of individuals of strange form among the meloid beetles make their collection an exciting experience. The flowers of the late-blooming composites, such as the scale-broom and the rabbit brush, often teem with them. They seem particularly fond of the flowers of the primroses and at times reduce great fields of them to bare stems in a few days. There is one particularly large species, *Lytta magister,* with red head and thorax, and black, pitted wing-covers which at times occur in such numbers on the gravelly mesas that a rasping sound fills the air about them. This noise is made by the scraping of the hard wing-covers against stones and dead vegetation as the beetles crawl awkwardly over the ground. I have found that the amber-colored blood of this insect is highly irritating when applied to the skin and will produce blisters in a few minutes. The greedy larvae probably feed on the eggs of grasshoppers.

The inflated beetle (*Cysteodemus armatus*), with much-arched wing-covers, crawls among the flowers and adorns itself with yellow pollen. This often completely fills the pits in the wing-covers, and one is tempted to think some protection is gained by this camouflage. We frequently see lone individuals on the sands, bustling about with all the appearance of being in a dreadful hurry and about to impart some important news to their fellows.

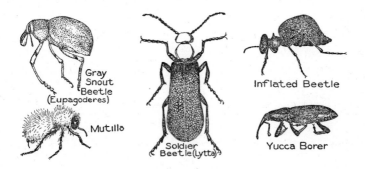

Gray Snout Beetle (Eupagoderes)

Mutilla

Soldier Beetle(Lytta)

Inflated Beetle

Yucca Borer

The majority of desert bees are solitary species which make cells of resin and sand, which they mount on shrubs;

or they construct nests in burrows excavated by themselves or found as natural cavities in the soil. The cells are provisioned with a paste made of pollen and nectar, and on this the eggs are laid. The time of emergence of the young bees is remarkably synchronized with the blooming of the particular flowers on which they feed and there is thus a distinct succession of species with the advance of the floral season. The same moisture which stimulates plant growth initiates the development of the bees. Sometimes when rains are not favorable the larvae do not complete their development, and there are indications that under these conditions they may hold over in the immature stage for as many as five or six years. Like many desert animals, the bees avoid the heat of day for work. The average life of the adult bee is about six weeks. *Dianthidium, Anthidiellum, Anthidium, Colletes,* and *Ashmediella* are common genera of arid regions.

Those insects of plastic behavior, the ants, are well adapted to arid lands, since many of them get on perfectly well without recourse to drinking. They generally find sources of water and food in the seeds and insect larvae which seasonally appear. The most widespread and abundant ants are naturally the seed-eating or harvester ants, for it is these that have the most dependable sources of food.

The large crater-like nests of the black harvester ant (*Messor pergandei*) are found in great abundance, particularly on the Mohave Desert north of the Santa Fe Railroad. No matter how stony the soil is they are certain to appear; even the bleak stretches of desert pavement are nesting-sites for them if salt bushes are near at hand to furnish seeds. The small ants are shiny black, and all day long you may see the tiny workmen busily engaged in bringing up little stones from the underground tunnels or gathering seeds to store in their granaries. The seeds are taken below and hulled, and the rejected chaff is brought up and placed upon the outer edge of the crater-like nest.

Another harvester (*Messor andrei*) is also common. The nests of this ant are built on smooth ground and the craters consist mostly of the chaff of wild buckwheat and alfilaree. The thorax is brownish, but the other parts are shiny black.

Then there are the large and powerful harvesters belonging to the genus *Pogonomyrmex*. The bearded harvester (*P. barbatus*) has a black head and thorax, but the gaster (abdomen) is reddish. It, like many other desert ants, must frequently remove the accumulation of dust and sand from its body. Special combs on its forelegs are used for this purpose. These combs are in turn cleaned by passing them through curious, basket-like "beards" of long hairs on the under surface of the head. Radiating from the large gravel craters which reveal the location of the nests, long lines of workers may be seen going to and returning from the forage fields. Sometimes the lines are a handsbreadth in width and two hundred yards long. The ants work only during the day but in midsummer they are out by 4:00 A.M. Wide clearings, two to twelve feet in diameter, are made about the nest openings and even the paths are kept free from vegetation. When rains come, circles of grass often spring up from seeds left about the refuse heaps.

The occidental harvester (*P. occidentalis*) is a large, reddish ant building conspicuous mounds of pebbles. These mounds are from 4 to 12 inches high and from 2 to 3 feet in diameter, and have small, cleared spaces about them. The entrance to the underground repositories is generally near the base of the mound. The passageways are closed at night, and several guards remain on duty at the opening. This ant has two spine-like projections on the last portion of the thorax.

The remarkable honey-pot ants (*Myrmecocystus mexicanus*), which turn certain of their numbers into veritable living bottles of honey, may be recognized by their light amber-colored bodies. The nests are generally made in sandy places, but gravelly soils may also be chosen. I remember once coming upon a nest in the early morning, and, thinking it was a small colony because there were but three watchmen about the entrance, I ventured to open it. Before beginning excavations, I tapped the ground vigorously, and a great swarm of soldiers rushed out with amazing suddenness and began moving about with those excited strides so characteristic of the group. Inside I found the galleries fairly teeming with workers and numbers of repletes, as the ants which serve as living honey-reservoirs are called. These honey ants are highly insectivorous.

Those furry-backed insects which so energetically wander about on the sands, and which are known as fuzzy ants or cow-killers, are really solitary, parasitic wasps. Only the males bear wings. The largest one known from the California deserts is the satanic mutillid (*Dasymutilla satanus*), a rather robust insect whose back is adorned with a deep pile of reddish-orange hair. Mention must also be made of the sand wanderer (*Dasymutilla arenivaga*), a medium-sized, less showy species, having the body covered with hoary and yellow hairs. The small mutillid, known as the "little old man of the sands" (*Dasymutilla gloriosa*), stands in strong contrast to its more colorful relatives in having not only its black body but also its legs sparsely covered with long, white hairs.

The great majority of the butterflies seen on our deserts, such as the anise swallowtail and the alfalfa yellow, are also common near the coast. It is of interest to note that the chalcedon checkerspot, which in the coastal district shows black as its dominant color, is found locally on the desert with red predominating. Of the butterflies found only on the desert the great yellow, two-tailed papilio (*Papilio multicaudata*), confined to the northern Mohave, is the largest. A number of white-winged butterflies are not infrequently seen flying together: Becker's pierid (*Pieris beckeri*), whose larvae feed on bladder pod, is found on both deserts, but the other three whites are exclusively Mohavean species whose larvae feed on mustards. The southern marble (*Euchloe creusa lotta*), known by the remarkable green color on the underside of the secondary wings, the rare desert orangetip (*Anthecharis ceuthura*), and the California white (*Pieris sisymbrii*) are all early fliers and may be taken in late March and early April.

The larvae of that dear little desert dwarf, the chara checkerspot (*Melitea chara*), feeds on the beloperone and nothing else; it is therefore confined wholly to the Colorado Desert. It is the smallest of all the California checkerspots and is difficult to see unless the insects are flying in great numbers. The eggs of Neumoegen's checkerspot (*Melitea neumoegenii*), a Mohavean species, are laid in a single mass at the foot of the flower stems of the Mohave aster (*Aster abatus*). The young caterpillars start feeding on the dainty stamens of the flowers, but as they get stronger they feed on the petals and finally on the leaves.

The rufescent patch (*Chlosyne lacinia crocale*) is a striking black butterfly, local in California on the Colorado Desert, but widely distributed in Arizona, Texas, and New Mexico. The normal food plant is the sunflower. The dainty, juniper-feeding thecla (*Metoura siva juniperiana*), with bronzy-brown upper-wings and underparts of green, brown, and white, flies from mid-March to mid-April. Since it seldom leaves its food plant, you must beat the bushes to get it. It may fly up in the air, but you are certain to see it soon settling again.

The San Emigdio blue butterfly (*Plebjus emigdionis*) shows a remarkable purple sheen on its small, blue wings. It is a saltbush feeder and the under side of the wings, which show when the insect is at rest, exactly matches the gray color of the food plant. The small blue butterfly (*Philotes speciosa*) lays its eggs on *Oxytheca perfoliata,* and when they hatch the tiny larvae begin to devour the green food in the center of the spine-tipped bracts. After feeding is over, it curls around the stem and rests, appearing now for all the world like a little seed in the bottom of the stem-pierced cup. As the mature insects try to fly in the strong winds which prevail in the spring on the Mohave Desert they stay close to the ground. When they alight to rest they seek a sunny place on the sand. Then, hooking the three legs of one side to a pebble, they allow the wind to blow them over parallel to the ground, the position of least resistance. How very clever!

It is the small moths that excel in number of species. Let the traveler begin to collect the myriads of kinds that hover about and dash into his campfire or the glare of his auto light, and he will be amazed at their number and beauty. There is not a month of the year when the collector's ardor will not be rewarded. The pupal life of many of them is spent unseen under ground, but a few are conspicuous because of the peculiar pupal cases they hang on the desert plants. The larva of the creosote psyche or bag-worm builds a silken, cigar-shaped case ornamented with the tips of creosote leaves. This is carried about as the larva feeds. In this case

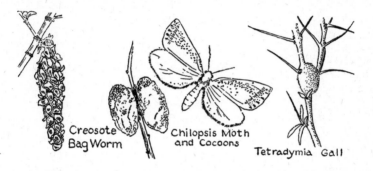

Creosote Bag Worm

Chilopsis Moth and Cocoons

Tetradymia Gall

it also pupates, and it is common to find the brown cocoons hung among the branches of the creosote bushes. Remarkable is the fact that the female, which develops in the case, never leaves the silken tube, even being fertilized there and laying her eggs within it. The larvae of the chilopsis moth (*Eucaterva variaria*) feed on the leaves of the desert willow and build meshed cocoons of tan-colored silk through which the pupae may be seen. These cases, which are hung high on the branches of the trees, appear like "wads of crumpled gauze," each about the size of a large olive.

Scorpions are found in all the warmer parts of the globe, being particularly partial to forests and arid wastes. Some 300 valid species, belonging to 56 genera, are known. As

with most poisonous animals, their ferocity and their poisonous nature have been much exaggerated. On warm nights
scorpions are frequently found crawling about in search of
insects and spiders, which are their chief food. If disturbed
they are always ready to assume a frightening attitude, and
when handled roughly bring their sting, found at the end of
the tail, into action. The poison is secreted by two glands
lodged in the sting. Although the wound is very painful, the
consequences are not serious. W. H. Wilson, experimenting
on desert animals in Egypt, found that they possessed a
degree of immunity to the venom of scorpions sufficient to
protect their lives from the fatal effect of the poison. In
parts of the piñon belt of eastern Nevada, where the ground
is covered with loose stones and fallen wood, I have esti-
mated the scorpion population to be several thousand to the
acre, but this density is exceptional. In early summer, the
young, which are born alive, may be seen, like the young of
wolf-spiders, mounted on the mother's back. Here, guarded
by her erect tail, they remain motionless until their first
moult, a time of about a week. During the daytime scorpions
lie concealed under rocks, in cracks of logs or in deep
excavations which they dig in loose soil. The entrance to
their underground retreat is a "flattish hole" running in at a
slight angle to the horizontal ground-surface. In front of
it there is always a small heap of earth.

Pseudo-scorpions are little brown creatures scarcely more
than an eighth of an inch long, appearing for all the world
like diminutive scorpions, except for the absence of a tail and
consequently a sting. They are found under rocks and under
bark and dead leaves, shunning the light. Normally when
disturbed they raise their claw-like pedipalps (so-called

hands) in most menacing fashion and then begin a backward retreat with short, jerky motions. They feed on small, soft-bodied insects and mites, and in winter hibernate in curious little round, flat nests built of silk and earth pellets. The silk is also made into cocoons for the eggs. A common desert genus is *Chelanops*.

Spiders, like ants, are more or less common wherever one goes. Only those of more specialized habits can contend successfully, however, with the rapid fluctuations in the abundance of insects on which they live. Those hairy monsters, the tarantulas, are most in evidence in the evenings or mornings of autumn and spring days when evidently they are engaged in a sort of migration. Hundreds may then be seen crossing the desert roads, sometimes all in the same direction. Though tarantulas bear poison in their cheliceral fangs, their bite is only moderately severe to persons in robust health. But why should anyone be bitten? Unless handled roughly, the tarantula is a quite harmless spider. He does not jump at you with intent to bite, and even his appearance is not so horrifying to you if you take a little intelligent interest in his ways.

There is a rather small, light-colored labyrinth spider (*Metepeira gosona*) that often appears in great numbers in autumn. It usually selects, by preference, the creosote bush for the site of the strong, irregular web which it stretches in generous style among the branches. Somewhere near the center of the net is hung a conspicuous, ragged, cylindrical retreat, made of silk and decorated with bits of dried leaves and sticks. It is about an inch and a half long, of the diameter of a pencil, and is the spider's daytime abode. In it the lens-shaped egg-cases are hung.

In late September in almost every creosote bush of certain districts of the Mohave Desert can be found a cylindrical, silken retreat about the size of the last joint of the little finger. It is unaccompanied by a web and is the home of a handsome, jumping spider, *Phidippus nikites.* This is a large, heavily built spider about half an inch long, for the most part black and with deep vermilion or salmon marks on the back of the abdomen and cephalo-thorax. The male runs about freely on the branches, but the female, which builds the retreat in which to hide the egg-case, is generally confined to a position near her silken domicile. The dainty-stemmed buckwheats, found in summer in such abundance about the borders of dry-type playas, are most excellent places to look for spiders of many species. One little spider (*Singa* sp.?) hangs her white, lentil-shaped egg-case in the forks of the stems and hides underneath it until the young emerge. These egg-sacs are often so plentiful that the plants holding them appear to be white with flowers.

Crab-spiders, belonging to the family *Thomisidae,* are fond of lurking in flowers. These spiders have the habit of moving with facility sidewise and backward as well as forward. A particularly interesting one is a flower-haunting species living in the flowers of the big white primrose (*Oenothera deltoides*), of the sand dunes. In her white and yellow garb, she lies in wait for honey-eating insects. The question is where she is and what she is doing during the long summer drought after all the primroses have dried to crispness.

To the lycosid spiders must be ascribed the curious little chimneys of sticks and silk which surmount the tops of the deep, tubular holes we so often see on the flat stretches of sand and clay. The taciturn, brown-bodied occupants spend their days at the bottoms of their burrows, venturing forth only at night for their insect prey.

The beautiful angelito (little angel) or desert velvet mite (*Trombidium magnificum*) is frequently met with on the sands after rains. It is a veritable little brocaded jewel, flashing its silken, scarlet body in the warm desert sunshine of spring. It is one of the largest of our harvest mites (one-quarter to one-third of an inch long), but in the African tropics there are even still larger ones measuring up to half an inch in diameter. The larvae are parasitic on insects.

Although in many places the amount of moisture and humus in the soil is almost imperceptible, there is frequently enough to make life possible for millipedes, those queer, brown, cylindrical, many-legged near-relatives of the centipedes. There are quite a number of strictly desert species found in the low desert mountains and intervening valleys. They not only tunnel beneath stones or go into the crevices of rocks but also go down the burrows of rodents or of insects or into excavations of their own digging. After rains, particularly at night, millipedes come forth to breed and to feed on decaying vegetation. Their presence on deserts is taken as an additional argument for the belief in a more humid past.

Visitors to the desert are usually in search of the bizarre among animals, and the active, night-moving, very spider-like vinegaroons or solpugids fulfill their wish for the unusual. If it is the summer season, the camper is almost certain in the morning to find one or more of the buffy-brown creatures hiding under his bed roll or other camping equipment. I once found five in my knapsack after a night's stay on the southern Nevada deserts. Though appearing so ferocious because of their enormous, powerful mandibles and long, constantly raised palps, vinegaroons are really quite harmless. Attracted by lights, they frequently invade tents and houses, where they run about with amazing speed, going, as it were, all over the place at once. If watched, they may be seen pouncing upon insects and crushing them with their extremely large jaws.

In the spring season, particularly at night, which is their time for roving, the soft, spherical-bodied granddaddy longlegs are busy scampering among the rocks or herbage. They are said to be very thirsty animals and to depend not alone on the colorless blood of their victims (the young of insects, spiders, and mites) for moisture but also upon water from dew drops or succulent plants. Under these conditions they must necessarily be conspicuously absent in the summer season. The desert species are probably short-lived, their day being co-terminous with the moist season. The eggs (twenty to forty laid by each female) are placed, without protection of cocoons, in cracks of the soil or under rocks or bark.

CHAPTER VI

SNAILS AND OTHER MOLLUSKS

BY S. STILLMAN BERRY

THE snails are certainly one group of animals which the unfamiliar mind is not likely to associate with deserts. Their soft bodies, composed so largely of water, are scarcely calculated to withstand rapid evaporation, and our hot rocks seem indeed a strange home for them. Yet search has shown that deserts in many parts of the world have their Mollusca, and that the elaboration of a quite extensive snail fauna has been the rule in such regions. It has been interesting to discover in recent years that our North American deserts form no exception to this rule.

It is not in loose soils or upon the arid floor of the desert that one looks for land snails, but in the rock slides and among loose rubbish on the slopes of the sere rocky hills which are so characteristic of the major desert topography. These snails are vegetable feeders. By means of a rasping organ found in the mouth they are able to scrape for food bits of plants growing in the crannies of the rocks. Since such food is found mostly in the spring season, this is the time of active feeding. Defense against the seemingly inhospitable environment is accomplished in none of our forms by any marked change of structure. Such adaptations as exist more often appear to be either physiological or arrived at through the accentuation of the shy, secretive habits so common to these animals. We find the desert snails developing a thicker, more opaque, and lighter-colored shell, taking on the habit of delving deeper into places of hiding and indulging in an exaggerated form of the normal powers of aestivation. When drought presses hard the animal withdraws into its shell and goes into a quiescent or torpid state in which it is able at the lower level of respiration and other life activities to continue its existence without nutriment or moisture for extended periods of time. Stearns has reported an instance of a Lower California land snail (*Micrarionta*) in his museum cabinet surviving in this way without food for six years. To prevent drying up while in the dormant condition the animal, retreating farther into its shell, secretes a tough papery covering known as the "epiphragm," which effectually seals the aperture. Sometimes several successive epiphragms are built one behind the other. The outermost one is often incomplete, consisting merely of a ring attaching the margin of the shell-opening to some solid object, such as a stick of wood or the lower side of a stone. By this it may adhere so strongly that one breaks the shell in trying to pull it away from its hold. When on the return of moist conditions the animal is ready to resume activity, the dry epiphragms are softened and loosened and the snail crawls away. The circular whitish seals left on the rock faces are a common phenomenon in the rock slides and furnish one of the "signs" whereby the keen collector determines whether or not snails are likely to be present in any given rock heap.

Intimate study reveals that no matter how many species are found over the desert as a whole, all are plainly derived from a very few primary stocks. Possibly the original species were more wide-ranging forms at a time when ecologically the desert was more continuous than at present, and the snails were able to push their domain across regions now quite impassable to them. The retreat of the desert mountains through the slow self-burial of their slopes and the increasing desiccation of the widening desert floor brought about the isolation of the snails inhabiting them. As a consequence we find here a small colony, there a larger one, which has been separated away and prevented from admixture with the remainder and forced along an evolutionary path of its own. We believe, and the facts of nature appear to substantiate the concept, that where this isolation is imperfect or of relatively recent attainment we find one and the same species in full occupancy of adjacent hills and ranges, but where the isolation has endured over a sufficiently long period the separated stocks become increasingly unable to maintain complete identity. In time the distinction between them becomes tangible enough for us to refer to them as distinct species. In southern Arizona the making of species in this fashion has proceeded so far that in some districts not only does each mountain range possess its peculiar forms but in the case of deep-delving or sedentary types a given species or subspecies may be confined to a single canyon or in some cases almost to a single rock pile. In the California desert area such exploration as has been carried out does not indicate that things attain to quite that pitch, but nevertheless a very interesting series of forms is being brought to light, the mapping of which may in time enable us to draw some highly interesting conclusions as to paths of migration and possibly, too, something of the more recent changes which have taken place in desert geology and physiography. This, however, is in anticipation of a great deal more, as well as much more careful and exhaustive, work on the subject than has yet been done. At present we must admit that our knowledge is very much in the formative stage, and proper discrimination and recognition of the different races is far from easy.

In some of the desert ranges no snail life whatsoever has been detected, but the snails appear to be pretty generally present wherever the rocks and cover are suitable for them. All the larger forms found are without exception members of the great and widespread family *Helicidae*. At present they are commonly classified in three genera, which differ appreciably from one another in shell characters but still more anatomically. The great majority of our species belong, however, to a single genus, *Micrarionta*.[1] The species which from the locality it chances to inhabit is likely to be first noticed by the casual observer is the handsome *Micrarionta wolcottiana*, the dead shells of which occur scattered in considerable numbers over the lower slopes of the mountains adjacent to Palm Springs. The shell is about the size of a small hickory nut, a light waxen brown with a narrow encircling band of brown when taken alive but soon bleaching to a chalky white after the death of the animal and

---

[1] Indeed to a special group, *Eremarionta*, at present referred to the larger group as a subgenus.

exposure to the elements. The living snails are usually hidden in some deep retreat in the rocks, and our ingenuity and patience if not our physical strength are likely to be well taxed before we succeed in discovering them unless perchance we are so fortunate as to encounter a herd of them out for a morning crawl after a spring rain.

If one happens to be collecting in the Victorville region he will find abundant relics of land snails which are different from any of the foregoing in both the character of the shell and the anatomy. These belong to the very typically California genus *Helminthoglypta,* which is common enough almost everywhere throughout the less arid parts of the state but which a few years ago we never thought of as being a desert inhabitant as well. The different desert species of this group are much alike in their brownish, narrowly banded shells, covered with fine microscopic granulations. The smooth finish and waxy or porcellaneous luster so prettily developed in the Micrariontas are conspicuously absent here. Characteristic species are *H. fisheri* from the Panamint Mountains, *H. jaegeri* from the Ord Mountains, *H. graniticola* from the mountains to the east of Victorville, and *H. mohaveana* from the tumbled heaps of granite along the Mohave River. Many of these forms seem so closely related to some found in the San Bernardino Mountains and farther south that it does not seem possible they could have been separated from them very long, however isolated from the main range all these scattered hillocks to the north now appear to be. These desert mountains evidently were *Helminthoglypta* territory long ago and still stubbornly remain so. In fact we have found no *Micrarionta* in this part of the desert until we reach the Newberry Range. After we reach that area all is *Micrarionta,* and we have unearthed not one *Helminthoglypta* except in the Panamint Range, where we find the two genera occurring together. In the Colorado Desert we do not encounter *Helminthoglypta* at all except where the common coastal species (*H. tudiculata*) has pushed through the passes, as in Sentenac Canyon and the Whitewater country, or where one of the mountain forms has descended a canyon, as in Snow Creek.

A third interesting snail genus is the characteristically cordilleran *Oreohelix,* a single species of which with a carinate lenticular shell was discovered in our area by the author of this book near the summit of one of the highest peaks in the Mohave. It lives, however, at too great an altitude for us to call it a true desert snail.

Anyone traversing the floor of the desert in the neighborhood of Indio is sure to notice numerous white specks all through the soil. Upon closer examination these reveal themselves as pretty spiral shells, for the most part quite minute. They occur in untold myriads not only over the surface but as deep in the silty alluvium as one may care to dig. Since when empty they are lighter than the sand grains, one often finds these shells blown into small windrows or collected in little pockets in such numbers that they may be scooped up a handful or a box-full at a time. Though a cause of surprise and wonder to many, the reason for their presence is not far to seek. They are simply relics of the former abundant life of the ancient Lake Cahuilla, the history of which we have already traced (see page 17). We must regard them in the light of fossils but as of such late origin that they have almost the nature of Recent shells. In some areas we find not only the small spiral shells above noted but one or two species of flat discoid snails (*Planor-bidae*), and a large and a minute freshwater mussel, the two valves frequently being found in place together. Most of these species are no longer to be found living in the immediate vicinity of the fossils, but we do find two of the tiny ones (genus *Paludestrina*) alive in a few lingering springs and mountain rills, where they seem to have sought a last retreat. It is interesting to sort out a representative collection of the fossil forms of the more slender of these (*P. protea*), the extremes of which seem incredible as belonging to one species, yet attempts to separate them into soundly distinguishable races have not thus far been very fruitful.

The student quickly observes that many of the desert land snails have been given picturesque names in one way or another indicative of the spot where they were first found. Such are *Micrarionta borregoensis* from Borrego Valley, *M. morongoana* from Morongo Valley, *M. aquae-albae* from White Water Canyon, and *M. avawatzica* from the Avawatz Mountains.

CHAPTER VII

FISHES, FROGS, AND TOADS

EVEN the arid regions of the earth are not without their fishes. In the sunny waters of some of the tepid or hot springs (72° to 93° F.) of the Mohave Desert, in and near Death Valley, swim bluish-brown minnows of the genus *Cyprinodon*. The finding of fish in these isolated springs was a great surprise to the early travelers, and the uninformed of today still raise the question how they got there. In reply it must be said that these fish, now found in segregated waters, are probably relicts from an ancient stream system which in Pleistocene times, or later, connected these springs.

Recent studies show that, while there are minor differences which have developed during their long isolation, these fish probably came originally from common ancestors. Excepting one fish population from Ash Meadows, Nevada, all are considered to belong to the species *macularius*. Similar if not identical minnows are found in warm alkaline springs of the Salton Basin (Fish Springs, Dos Palmos). The Ash Meadow minnow, because of its darker color, small size, and the shape of the teeth, has been recently described as a new species (*C. diabolis*). In the different populations the characters vary with the temperature, the fish in hotter waters exhibiting the greatest differences. It is of interest to note that fish of this genus, *Cyprinodon,* live also in briny springs and hot pools of the Sahara and Dead Sea deserts. Like those living in our desert pools, some have suffered the modification or loss of their ventral fins.

When we turn to the consideration of the native fish of the Mohave River we find further evidence that the ancient streams of the Mohave Desert were integrated into a single river system, with Death Valley Lake acting as the important link that connected them. Two fishes now inhabit the Mohave River, the common introduced catfish (*Amiurus nebulosus*) and a native minnow (*Siphateles mohavensis*), the last closely related to a minnow of the Owens River (*S. obesus*). "It seems quite likely," says David Thompson, "that an ancestral form of *Siphateles obesus* which now inhabits Owens River may have traveled through the Owens–Death Valley system and through a permanent or temporary lake in Death Valley and entered the Mohave River basin where it became modified to the *S. mohavensis* form."

The fish that swim in the briny waters of the Salton Sea came in, for the most part, with the incursion of the Colorado River in 1905 and 1906. Some of them once occurred in quantities sufficient to tempt Portuguese fishermen to make a commercial venture of them. Among those now known to live there are the hump-backed sucker, the mullet, and the Colorado River trout. Carp, once so abundant, have disappeared. The small desert cyprinodont and another minnow (*Gambusia affinis*) are common along the shallow shore waters.

Our desert's toad and frog fauna is a limited one. Except for the species inhabiting the Colorado River and connecting streams, the explanation of their interrupted and limited distribution is found in remembering that in those more humid days that prevailed in the geologic past there were means of dispersion which, to animals so wedded to water as the frogs and toads, are no longer available.

The red-spotted toad (*Bufo punctatus*) is a species confined wholly to the deserts of southwestern United States and northern Mexico. It is restricted to canyons where permanent seepage and springs occur. The best field-marks other than its diminutive size (it is less than three inches long) are the small, squat, vermilion-tipped warts, that appear like handsome jewels, on its back. Spawning takes place in April and the toads may then be heard in loud song, adding new notes to the chorus of spring. The cricket-like voice is long-continued and shrill. The little gray throat swells out into a rounded pouch-like sack; "just like he had swallowed a marble," said an old prospector. These toads are for the most part nocturnal, hiding during the day in rock crevices on the borders of the streams and spring basins.

The Pacific tree toad (*Hyla regilla*) is a hardy little creature of greenish hue, scarcely more than two inches in length. The best field-marks for the use of the novice are the adhesive pads on the fingers and toes and the dark stripe along the side of the head. This toad is widely distributed on the Pacific Coast and in many points of the desert, except in the extreme southeastern portion. The cry of the males, "Kreck-rk," uttered over and over again in rapid succession, is always good evidence of the full approach of spring. The adults hide, not in trees as the name would imply, but in rock crevices and under vegetation about the springs. In the evening they shamble forth on the banks, intent upon snapping up insects.

The drab livery of the sand-colored tree toad (*Hyla arenicolor*) is an adaptation apparently physiological. It is always some tone of gray with close resemblance to the granite bowlders, among the crevices of which the animal rests. This is its means of defying detection, for it appears, indeed, more like a mere "bump on a rock." The species is one from desert canyons carrying perennial streams, and there one often hears the murmurous music of the male. The notes are made with the mouth held wide open.

CHAPTER VIII

REPTILE LIFE

LIZARDS are perhaps the most conspicuous and the most frequently seen animals of our deserts. Summer travelers are particularly interested in them because of the numbers they see on the pavements of the desert roads and are not less surprised at the speed that some of them show when frightened by the approach of the motor car.

Appearing for all the world like some small, slender-bodied, gray-white mammal, the crested or keel-backed lizard (*Dipsosaurus dorsalis*) dashes wildly across the glaring sands, stopping only when he considers himself far beyond reach. Then, turning around, he raises himself high on stilted limbs and gazes at his pursuer, ready at a moment's notice to continue his flight to some other position of safety. On the southern deserts individuals are out as early as March. They then may be seen in pairs playing about or basking in the sun on old prostrate ironwood logs of the sandy washes. On the Mohave Desert they do not come from their winter retreats in the sand until fully a month later. The general color is tawny brown or grayish, with darker bars and spots running both longitudinally and transversely. When they are angered, reddish-brown circles appear on their backs. One taken on the dunes of the Amargosa Desert of Nevada measured more than two feet in length, fully half of which was tail. As it was in winter,

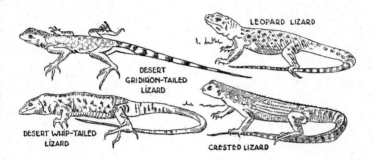

LEOPARD LIZARD

DESERT GRIDIRON-TAILED LIZARD

DESERT WHIP-TAILED LIZARD

CRESTED LIZARD

when food was very scarce, the lizard's leathery skin hung shaggily over its gaunt frame. This grotesque lizard is unique in having a dorsal crest or comb of strongly keeled scales, beginning just at the back of the head and running almost the length of the tail. As the animal raises itself on its limbs to run, the scales are erected, giving it a most formidable appearance. It lives about the dunes, generally seeking protection in burrows under shrubs and mesquite trees. Like the chuckawalla, the keel-backed lizard is able to inflate its body in order to prevent its enemies from extracting it from the crevices or holes in which it has sought safety. During the heat of the day we may find it feeding on flowers or on the leaves of such small shrubs and trees as it can climb.

At that time of late spring when the sands are dazzling under the white rays of the desert sun and the ephemeral flowers are giving way under a wilting dryness, the gridiron-tailed lizard (*Callisaurus ventralis*) is making itself evident in almost every sandy waste. It is the season of mating, and even the murderous callisaurus is feeling the impulse of love. Again and again I have seen pairs of them going through the fancy curves of the courting dance, waltzing back and forth in curious frolics like a pair of amorous mocking birds. The movements, full of pleasing grace and weird rhythm, are engaged in for long periods. On such occasions gridiron-tailed lizards may be approached with ease, but on all others they are excessively wild. While hunting, it carries its slender body close to the ground with the tail curled up at the end; but let an individual be alarmed and it raises itself and runs away with full enjoyment of its vigorous powers of flight and at incredible speed. When finally it stops, the animal turns around and steadily gazes at its pursuer in a wild, resentful manner, with head and shoulders raised high and limbs held ready to speed on at a moment's notice. If hard pressed it dives out of sight in the sand or retreats into rodent holes with a cleverness that must outwit the most wily pursuer. The gridiron-tailed lizard is a greedy feeder and often snaps up the smaller lizards as his legitimate prey, swallowing the recalcitrant victims alive. Other food consists of insects and the buds and green leaves of the desert herbs. The black bands which adorn the tail vary in number from four to eight and are always a conspicuous means of identification. The body takes on the whitish color of the silver sands so that it is often impossible to see the lizard until it starts on its mad dash to safety. Two brilliant, bluish-black bars ornament the sides of the body of the males.

Another successful candidate for notoriety as a runner is the desert whiptailed lizard (*Cnemidophorus tigris*). A momentary glimpse is all we may obtain of the swift moving form as it skims over the sands on a burning midsummer day. It seems to maintain itself in a perpetual state of alertness and generally eludes us even on our most vigilant chases. Familiar with its strength, and as if playing some sort of game, it keeps just far enough ahead to be out of reach. The stalker of this wary lizard must manifest the greatest self-control. In order to frustrate his designs, it often dives into the shelter of a bush, where it may mask its presence among the shadows of the branches. These swift-jacks, as they are sometimes called because of their rapidity of movement, have, while hunting, the curious habit of creeping jerkily over the sands, at the same time thrusting out their tongues. I recently saw one behaving after this manner and was surprised to find it later using its forefeet for digging, a habit common enough among mammals but rather unique among lizards. A single foot was brought into play, while it kept watch for the object of its search—a small, burrowing insect.

The leopard lizard (*Crotaphytus wislisenii*) is, like its gridiron-tailed cousin, a denizen of the broad stretches of the sandy mesas and washes of the open desert. In spite of its large body it is capable of great speed and if caught in disadvantageous positions is able to give its pursuer a merry and prolonged chase before being taken. The hotter the day the more interesting and racy the pursuit. When undisturbed this lizard spends much time skulking about in the flecking shadows of the low desert shrubs around and upon which it finds much of its food. The silver-winged grasshopper,

singing in the creosote bushes, is often snatched from its
perch by a leaping crotaphytus, which may have jumped
three times its own length to get it. In Pinto Basin in Riverside County I caught a large male swallowing a crested
lizard almost his own size. Strange to say, the two-thirds–
devoured saurian, though wounded about the head, soon
recovered when spewed from the mouth of his cannibalistic
cousin and before long seemed as lively as ever. The diet
of the leopard lizard is varied by eating blossoms and leaves
of herbaceous annuals.

The ocellated sand-lizard (*Uma notata*) with peculiar,
blotched markings, is limited to the sandy wastes and dunes
along the Mohave River and territory contiguous to the
Colorado River. You are certain to see it on the Algodones
Dunes near Yuma. It is very wary, a swift runner, and has

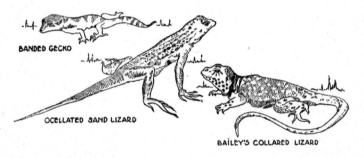

BANDED GECKO

OCELLATED SAND LIZARD

BAILEY'S COLLARED LIZARD

the remarkable habit of burying itself beneath the sand when
pursued, leaving only a puff of dust as evidence of its place
of retreat. When flushed from its hiding it makes a rapid
dash across the open, to secrete itself again. A curious adaptation to its habitat is seen in the fringes of elongate scales
which broaden the toes and increase its ability to burrow

and also to run rapidly over the loose sands. Its food consists of insects—ants, beetles, bees, grasshoppers—and the leaves of herbaceous annuals.

The chuckawalla (*Sauromeles ater*) is California's largest native lizard and most bizarre in form. A full-grown individual may reach a length of eighteen inches and have a body four inches wide. This is a rock-loving species, seldom found in open sandy spaces. When the sun is blazing hot, chuckawallas become most lively. Though their bodies are of obese proportions, they are clever at dodging and when pressed by a pursuer they may run at considerable speed. The chase is generally ended when the lizard darts into a deep rock-crevice and inflates its body so greatly that it is impossible to extract it. When caught in open places, chuckawallas defend themselves by long, lashing strokes of the tail, or they may resort to biting. I am well aware through experience that the teeth of a full-grown adult are capable of inflicting painful wounds.

The chuckawalla is a thoroughgoing vegetarian. During the days of spring it is a greedy feeder on flowers and it even climbs into small shrubs to get them. Several times I have seen one high up among the fat stems of the brittle-bush, snapping with heavy jaws at the yellow blossoms. When flowers are not available, both leaves and green stems are eaten. Even such bitter, aromatic shrubs as the burro-weed and the creosote bush are not shunned.

During winter and also at night, retreats are sought in deep rock-crevices. When spring opens, chuckawallas come forth lean and gaunt and are often too weak to run. Under such conditions they are easily snapped up by birds of prey, which doubtless prize them as food for nestling young.

The body-color and pattern vary considerably in different individuals. The finely beaded skin is often grayish-brown, dark-brown, or black, with markings of red-brown. The fat, scaly tail is often white or light gray and girdled by broad, black bands.

Sooner or later, when turning over stones, you will come upon the gentle banded gecko (*Coleonyx variegatus*), a little lizard of handsome color and pleasing manner. The loose skin has an almost waxy appearance, while the upper surface varies in color from yellowish to fawn, relieved by the beautiful walnut-brown transverse bands of the back and tail. The peculiar, small, fleshy spurs on the sides of the tail near its root are certain to arouse our interest. A full-grown adult measures about four inches in length. The curious habit of emitting a feeble, squeaking noise when disturbed is always a delightful surprise to the listener. Often the timid creature opens its mouth as if yawning, then proceeds to lick its jaws, like a little dog that has just finished a meal. When it desires to move it raises itself on its weak limbs with the aid of its tail, presenting a picture of helplessness which almost arouses in one an emotion of compassion.

The beautiful giant uta (*Uta mearnsi*) is confined largely to the west side of the Colorado Desert, where it frequents the bowlders and vertical rock walls of the deep mountain gorges. In the low mountains west of Brawley, it is the commonest lizard seen. It is sometimes confused with Bailey's collared lizard because of the presence of the narrow band of intense black between its shoulders. When, however, the two lizards are compared, the difference at once becomes obvious: Mearns's uta has a single, black shoulder-band, while Bailey's lizard has two. It is extraordinarily shy and when approached quickly runs beyond reach or hastens to conceal itself. When caught it attempts to defend itself by biting. Hunting goes on all through the day, but there is less activity when the heat becomes intense. So clever are the maneuvers in stalking the insect prey that I have passed away many a pleasant hour watching them boldly leaping from rock to rock or creeping along granite surfaces to get into positions most advantageous for capturing the insects they were stalking. The vision must be keen, for I have seen them commence their stalking movements when more than five feet from a fly.

The desert brown-shouldered lizard (*Uta stansburiana elegans*) is such a lively little creature and such a frequent visitor to the environs of our desert camps that we cannot but feel it is our choice from among all our saurian neighbors. Acting the host, we are inclined to invite it to our premises and give it permission to catch all the flies it can get without fear of molestation. Of all its peculiar antics there is none more engaging than that of spasmodically bobbing the body as it nervously fidgets about while stalking its winged insect-prey. In the breeding season the metallic-blue spots on its sides are very conspicuous and give an added charm to the mottled, brownish-gray coat of this little saurian aristocrat of the desert rocks.

The small, long-tailed uta (*Uta graciosa*), conspicuous because of its extraordinarily long tail, is a denizen of the desert bordering the Colorado River. "Long-tailed utas like to sun themselves," says Dr. Camp, "on the topmost twig of a bush, hanging motionless and head downwards as though pinned there by a shrike. If disturbed they drop to the middle of the bush and flatten themselves against a limb lengthwise, keeping on the side away from the intruder, their wiry tails stretched out stiffly in line with the body. When alarmed while on the ground they make for the nearest bush and jump into it, there to dodge actively about among the branches, quite unlike their brown-shouldered relatives, which usually retreat beneath stones or into holes when pursued."

In California the beautifully marked Arizona tree uta (*Uta ornata symmetrica*) occurs only among the wooded bottoms of the Colorado River between Yuma and Needles, but in Arizona it is widely distributed from the Grand Canyon to the southern borders of the state. It may be distinguished from the desert brown-shouldered lizard, which to the uninitiated it in many ways resembles, by the presence of the longitudinal dorso-lateral skin-fold and by the absence of the rounded, blue blotch behind the axilla. It spends much of its time climbing over the bark of the willows and other river-bottom trees, seeking for insects.

Those who are curious to see the wide-awake desert night lizard (*Xantusia vigilis*) will find it hiding in holes and crevices of decaying yucca stems. When first brought out into the light it seems dazed but soon shows signs of life and attempts by means of its diminutive legs to get away to a place of hiding. The smoky-gray color of the body blends perfectly with the peculiar setting in which Nature intended it to be seen. If handled at all roughly, the small, timid creature generally drops the tail, leaving it to squirm out of the hand and slither over the ground. Termites, which probably constitute its principal food, are hunted at night.

The desert scaly lizard (*Sceloporus magister*) is a rather large, heavily-built saurian with prominent scales over most of its body. Its spiny armor adapts it to move with ease among the bushes where it resides. Individuals are often seen climbing about wood-rats' nests, in cactus bushes, and in mesquite trees. Theirs is a mixed diet, but insects are their principal fare. The males are brightly colored in the breeding season; at that time the ordinary, mottled, gray-green body becomes ornamented, especially in the neck region, with shades of orange, blue, yellow, and brown. This lizard is more or less common over the entire southwestern desert area.

The flat-nosed horned lizard (*Phrynosoma platyrhinos*), with short head-spines, is the only horned lizard of the Mohave region. On the Colorado Desert we find, with it, the flat-tailed horned lizard (*Phrynosoma m'callii*), a species armed with large head-spines and with ashy-gray body bearing a narrow but distinct line down the center of the back. The food of these squat reptiles consists of insects, among which ants are a favorite. During the coolest months of the year they secrete themselves in the sand.

Not long will you wander about before you see living specimens or at least old bleached pieces of the bony carapace of the desert tortoise (*Gopherus agassizi*). Time was when this reptile was common in the Salton Basin; this is unhappily no longer the case. Their food is green plant material and this accounts for the apparent frequency of tortoises during the spring months. In winter as well as during the hottest summer months, they hide beneath rocks, or dig slanting burrows two or three feet deep in the sand. In the making of the retreat the earth is scraped loose with the forefeet, whereupon the animal turns around and pushes it out with its shoulders. To enable it to withstand periods of drought the tortoise stores water in a pair of sacs situated between its flesh and its "shell." Numbers of tortoises are killed yearly by thoughtless autoists, and as many more are transported by curious folk to the coastal towns, where the animals live for a while in their new environment and then perish.

Snakes are by no means common desert reptiles. They are found most often in the spring of the year, which is their mating season. A number of kinds are seen only at night, and this accounts for the scarcity of records of their occurrence. It is a great mistake to think that desert snakes are partial to sunshine and that they make no attempt to avoid the burning heat. Some of them, such as the horned rattlesnake, are killed by exposure to the hot sun for only a short time.

The common olive-green rattlesnake of the open country of the Mohave Desert is the Mohave rattler (*Crotalus scutulatus*). It comes from its winter retreats early in March and is in evidence all through the summer. Its activities are not confined to the daylight hours, but it crawls at night, taking kangaroo rats and other small rodents which are then about. In the rock-mantled mountains of the northern Mohave Desert (Inyo, Coso, Panamint, Slate, Grapevine, and Funeral Mountains) occurs the Panamint rattlesnake (*Crotalus confluentus stephensi*). The general ground color of this snake is tan, buff, or gray, with considerable variation occurring in the different mountain ranges. As early as the last of March, individuals are out sunning themselves on the rocks.

The Texas rattlesnake (*Crotalus atrox*) is largely restricted to the Coachella and Imperial valleys and the region along the Colorado River near Yuma. It is a grayish or yellowish-brown species inhabiting the sandy-bottomed basins. In the rocky, mountainous areas in this same region the big yellow or pallid rattlesnake (*Crotalus mitchelii*) is encountered. This snake is also a Mohavean species.

Both in the broad, unicolorous, sandy basins and on the stony deserts of low altitude, the little horned rattlesnake or sidewinder (*Crotalus cerastes*) must be reckoned with by

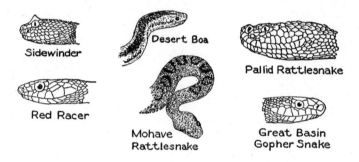

Sidewinder

Desert Boa

Pallid Rattlesnake

Red Racer

Mohave Rattlesnake

Great Basin Gopher Snake

those travelers who roam about or camp on the desert at night. During the daytime this small but hot-tempered snake lies coiled in pits of sand or in small depressions about the shady bases of bushes where it has protection from the inhospitable sun. About sunset it begins to wander extensively in search of its prey, which consists mostly of wild mice and lizards. It moves in a singular sidewise, looping manner and leaves behind a series of telltale tracks in the loose soil. I often have been surprised to find sidewinders out on cold, windy days of early March and mid-November, weather which to other reptiles is most discouraging to activity.

Excepting the red racer and the desert gopher snake, few of the snakes enumerated as non-poisonous are seen alive by the average traveler. The desert burrowing snake, the patch-nosed snake, and the California boa are sometimes seen dead on the highways as the result of auto casualties.

CHAPTER IX

BIRDS

THROUGHOUT the spring flower-season the whole desert country is one broad food table for the birds. The tired bird-migrants, stopping for a few days' rest at the springs before going farther north, feed fat on the insects and ripening seeds, while the native nesting birds, assured of a full larder on which to draw while hatching their eggs and feeding their young, are busy preparing nests or engaging arduously in nursery duties. It is a fact well worth noting that during the drought years when there is little promise of food supplies many of the desert birds, such as the insect-eating cactus wren and the thrashers, full of avian wisdom, nest early, or cut down the number of eggs, or forego both nesting and egg-laying, passing over the season without offspring.

About the springs and the small streams which trickle from them, one quickly ceases to be surprised at new bird visitors. A position of great advantage to the watcher of birds is the lone spring with its overhanging willow or two affording some semblance of protection to small birds from their rapacious and unloved brothers, the hawks. Twenty or more different kinds of birds a day in the month of April (the height of the migratory season) constitute no small list of waterhole visitants, yet the bird lover frequently sees that many. A good big pillow to lean the elbow on, some lunch, a pair of eight-power field glasses, and a large share of patience make a combination that surely brings great rewards. Goldfinches (the willow, the Lawerance, and the greenback), linnets, house wrens, mourning doves, mocking birds, Alaska yellow warblers, hermit thrushes, and even the ever-contented red-shafted flicker are sure to be seen sooner or later. Running about on the rocks, almost like a mouse, that voluble, merry, scale-running songster, the canyon wren and his near relative, the less musical but persistently singing, joyous-hearted rock wren, are perhaps watching for insects and spiders, quite oblivious or at least inattentive to their many bird neighbors below. By late April the sky is emptied of most of the fleeting migrants and there are left such hardy, endemic birds as the Say's phoebe, the raven, the roadrunner, the horned lark, the Gambel quail, the white-rumped shrike, the verdin, the plumbeous gnatcatcher, and the Le Conte and Crissal thrashers, those true sons of the desert which are able to go for long periods without dipping their beaks in water. During certain seasons some of them which are seed-eaters depend largely for their supply of moisture on the water found in the leaves of succulent plants or berries. Others, like the raven and the roadrunner, get quantities of water from the bodies of lizards and dead rabbits; but most of them secure water by eating insects or by elaborating it in their own bodies through the processes of metabolism. The amount of this metabolic water is probably not great, certainly not as great as develops in many of the rodents. Most birds take water at the springs and rivers when they can procure it, but apparently get along for long periods without recourse to the watering-places when they must do so. It is always to be remembered, however, that birds are not infrequently aware of small sources of water of which their human admirers never know. Also, many of them travel longer distances to water than one would dare to expect. Bolster tells of the sand grouse (*Pterocles senegallus*), which is a bird of the bare Old World deserts and in need of daily supplies of water, breeding at least thirty miles from the pools from which it drinks. The parents carry water to the young by saturating their breast plumage, and the young pass their bills through the feathers to procure the bits of water.

The few marshes and the narrow, muddy margins of the isolated springs, lakes, and rivers offer attractions to many of the wading birds. Terns, stilts, avocets, grebes, kingfishers, cormorants, ibises, and many kinds of ducks in their season of migration are drawn by the opportunity to feed and rest in such agreeable surroundings as they find at Saratoga Springs, by the Salton Sea, and along the bottoms of the Colorado River.

The great, domed saltbushes of the Salton Sink offer such ideal shelter and feeding-grounds for the roadrunner that I am always sure of a sight of half a dozen or more of these amusing birds in any morning's ramble there. One of the cleverest exhibits of roadrunner sagacity came to me last winter. Approaching one of those dried mud puddles of the roadside so common near Mecca, I saw George, as I like to call him, turning over the big mud plates which, curled up about the edges, lay all over the surface of the old mud pool. Catching hold of them with his beak, he turned them up on end, and over, all the time on the lookout for crickets and other insects which were lying hidden beneath. It was evidently an old trick of his, for all the mud plates on that and another pool had been turned. One is led to ask if he had taken lessons from his bird cousins, the turnstones and ovenbirds, or if he himself had invented this novel way of getting at new sources of food.

Gambel Quail   Roadrunner   Scott Oriole   Desert Sparrow

In company with two of my students I saw, on a recent midsummer morning's jaunt, a roadrunner making great haste to get to the shelter of a creosote bush. Two somber-colored marsh hawks were after him. Contrary to what I expected, the hawks lighted on the ground and began making repeated dives into the creosote bush. The roadrunner did not long stay under cover, for he was no coward. A moment later we saw him become the aggressor in the struggle. Then and there began a merry tussle, both hawks and roadrunner going in more or less merry-go-round fashion around the bush, the hawks rather awkwardly, the roadrunner very gracefully. The latter, seemingly, was enjoying the contest enormously. At length one of the hawks retreated to some distance, but the other flew away and alighted under a creosotc bush that was close at hand. George immediately went over to him, for he was not through with his fun, and there began all over again the ludicrous dodging and running back and forth around the bush. Finally outdone in the contest of wits, the last hawk disgustedly flew away. The triumphant roadrunner, with head held proudly aloft and with a clipping of its bill, ran off unconcernedly at top speed.

The small ladder-backed or Texas woodpecker is a noisy little fellow, often calling in high-pitched notes as he flies in undulating sweep from bush to bush. Before the advent of civilization he drilled his nest-holes in the tree yuccas, in cactus stems, and in branches of larger trees when he could find them. With the coming of the railroads and the power lines he found new materials for his beak to drill in. The erection of telegraph, telephone, and power-line poles was a stroke of good luck for him. He at once took to drilling so many holes that he made himself a creature of concern. Thousands of poles have been ruined by his innocent work.

Except perhaps for a few weeks in the spring when there are succulent plants in abundance and quantities of berries on the bushes of the wild Lyciums, the Gambel quail is a daily drinker and thus pretty closely confined to the vicinity of springs and streams. This handsome bird is found not only on the desert floor but also in the stony canyons high up among the junipers and piñons.

Another interesting avian resident is the buoyantly flighted Say's phoebe, a flycatcher of general gray-brown color with parts underneath tending toward rusty. It is one of the few birds to be seen in the lowest parts of Death Valley and other places where the more extreme types of desert conditions prevail. Very early in the morning, long before the sun is up, its plaintive and haunting but forceful songs are heard in great numbers. As soon as the birds are able to see well, there is a noticeable surcease of song. Then for an hour or more they may be seen actively foraging for insects, making repeated sallies from some isolated cliff or fence post out into mid-air to capture their flying breakfast. But before

the morning is half over the songs are heard again. The birds continue their calls until evening, except at noonday, when they take refuge from the heat under bushes or rock ledges. Almost every abandoned miner's shack has its phoebe's nest on some rafter. The nest, often built on some ledge of an abandoned mine shaft, is made of old string, grass, and bits of paper. A pair of the birds once nested for me in a rusty stovepipe; this they half filled with bits of string and manure. It was on the sunny side of the house and in the month of May. How the birds kept themselves from roasting alive is still a mystery to me.

To that stolid old-gentleman-tramp of the railway right-of-way, the raven, time is no object. He and his mate may be seen, even during the scorching days of summer, walking or flying with a business-like demeanor up and down the railroad tracks, alert to find the morsels that are thrown from lunch baskets or dining-car trays. At times the raven seems a dull, inactive creature, but he really has a great share of curiosity and something of a sense of humor; I believe his ways deserve careful study. It is noteworthy that this sagacious bird, though so large, has been able to survive his many persecutors. On the rocky deserts he gets his supplies of water by eating insects, bird's eggs, lizards, or the carcasses of rabbits that have been killed on the motor highways. It is probable that along the Colorado River he not only gets a good drink but also a fish occasionally.

The English sparrow, our almost universal bird scamp, has followed the sun westward and penetrated even to the bottom of Death Valley. There he chirps disquieting songs to the small birds which with him seek protection under the downhanging leaves of the Washingtonia palms at Furnace Creek Ranch. The English sparrow has this redeeming trait: he confines himself to the vicinity of human habitations.

Among the really fine singers of spring is the desert sparrow. His song is a quaint but cheerful and far-carrying melody *"tsee tsi tsi tsi tsee* or *weet weet wee,* the last note held and almost trilled."* Approach him closely and you can see his well-defined, black chest and chin and the distinctive, clean, white lines above and below his eye. The nest, built of plant fibers, is placed in low shrubs or in crotches of the spiny opuntias.

Like a glad harbinger of the glorious, sunny, winter days to come, the Gambel white-crowned sparrows appear from the north early in November to make their home in the Salton Sink. The birds are soon everywhere, filling the air with their simple, cheerful songs, sometimes seemingly singing in chorus. They are joined soon after by Audubon warblers, by Western or mountain bluebirds, robins, linnets, and a host of obscurely marked sparrows such as the sage sparrow and the bell sparrow. We see many of the sparrows consorting in flocks to go wheeling about in the air or gathering in small groups to feed in very businesslike manner about the bases of bushes where seeds of the summer's ripening have been collected by the winds. Some days when storms occur in the mountains Thurber juncos and Bailey chickadees come down to join the merry company.

The cactus wren, by reason of its clattering call notes and queer, flask-shaped nests which it builds in cactus bushes and in palo verde trees, is one of the most conspicuous of desert birds. It is always interesting to examine a fresh nest to see what plants have been chosen for use in its construction and decoration. The fine-stemmed eriogonums and the woolly filagos and styloclines are almost always present; sometimes a few bright-hued blossoms are added to the outside, apparently as a decoration.

Pleasant indeed it is to wake up in the morning and hear the little rock wren merrily greeting the dawn with its absurd but merry, tinkling song. Watch persistently among the barren ledges of the rocky hills near by and you will see it perched on the summit of some bowlder or spit of rock, bobbing up and down like an ouzel. Later you may see the shy little creature retreating into piles of loose rocks, where it hunts its insect food and rears its young. If it is autumn its coat of brown feathers will be much worn: a season of constant activity in the rocky retreats has surely left its mark.

The desert claims the finest-singing and the handsomest of California's orioles. The trim black-and-yellow Scott oriole is a regular resident of the yucca forests of the Mohave Desert, and occasionally it is found flashing its brilliant form among the junipers. Its fibrous nest is fastened to the stiff spines of the yuccas. In the Colorado Desert the Arizona hooded oriole hangs its nest in the palms.

The little ball of gray twigs you so often see in the mesquite branches or in the spiny cat's-claw thickets is the nest of the tiny but active verdin. If the owner is anywhere about, you are certain to hear its insistent *tzee*-ing notes. Verdins always appear to be provident birds, and very much in earnest in whatever they do. Early in the season we see them engaging all their energies in collecting and bringing in the material for the new home. Often it is made from feathers and sticks from the previous year's nest. The male has the curious habit of building a separate sleeping nest. He is in some respects a lazy chap, and you will observe that his house is not as well constructed or as neatly furnished as is the nest of his mate. In winter you may occasionally see him pop into his nest before sundown. Put your finger in through the small opening and you are certain to get a sharp pick. The verdin's yellow head, his chestnut-red shoulder patches, and the contrasting gray of the other parts of his body are field marks matched by no other desert bird.

Often in small companies, but more frequently in pairs, the Yuma horned larks wander about in the open valleys, always protected by the plain browns and grays of their plumage. The furnace-like heat of glaring, alkaline plains and scorching sand dunes holds no terrors for them and we need not be surprised to find a female in late spring nesting in a depression of sand beside some clump of bunch grass and with nearly the minimum of shelter from the garish sun.

Disturb her and she flies a little way across the heat-scarred soil, circles around anxiously, and, with beak agape, soon returns and settles on her eggs.

No lazy birds are the gnatcatchers. Always hustling about in a great deal of excitement, they are certain to claim our attention, particularly if it is early spring when they have nesting duties. The commonest desert species is the lead-colored gnatcatcher, especially plentiful in the mesquite thickets of the Colorado Desert. The call notes, a series of two or three short *chees,* are given as the birds in pairs work their way from bush to bush. One generally takes the lead, and the other, seemingly much excited, soon follows. Its tail is never still but is continually flipped from side to side.

In the topmost twig of some mesquite or ironwood tree you are certain, sooner or later, to see that feathered bird-aristocrat, the glossy, black phainopepla. In all probability he will, by the motions of his proud head, display his fine black crest and scarlet eye or, flying gracefully upward after some insect, will reveal the remarkable white patches of the under wing-feathers. In the clump of mistletoe beneath him are those pearly-white or pinkish berries which he relishes above all foods. On twigs and on posts near at hand you see the evidences of his keen appetite, the high heaps of rejected, sticky seeds which passed undigested through his body.

Another feathered inhabitant that never seems to mind the heat nor, we may say incidentally, his own business, is the neatly attired, white-rumped shrike. Were it not for his flattened head, which gives him the appearance of a creature of low intelligence, we should call him a handsome bird. From earliest dawn we hear his sharp cries and, if it is near the nesting season, his song may have in it an element of beauty, for even this cruel-hearted bird, which pins little birds on barbed-wire fences and mesquite thorns, is, in the days of his love, no longer the harsh-voiced fellow he was in late summer or winter. If you would have some real excitement co-mingled with an element of fun, hunt out a nest of young shrikes at just about the time when they are leaving it. The hubbub of excited cries and screeches from the baby birds and the noisy, daring dashes of the anxious parents, which seem ready to deliver stabs and blows fatal to the intruder, will never be forgotten. Inasmuch as shrikes feed on insects and get most of their water from this source, they are not dependent on the water holes and springs but scatter widely over the desert basins throughout the year.

The wise traveler will always get up early in the morning with the rock wrens and catch the changing glories of the coming day. Also he will learn to spend the closing hours of the day in quietness so as to have full opportunity to watch the setting sun, the cloud forms which it gilds and reddens, and perchance to hear, in contrast to the intense stillness of evening, the clear, liquid notes of that magnificent bird singer of the mesquite country, the Le Conte thrasher. The song of this ashy-gray bird with its long curved beak is remarkable for the richness of its tones. It is much like that of the mocking bird but less formal. Quite in contrast is the call note or note of alarm, a sharp whistle— *whit*. This is the desert's shyest bird and when disturbed by an intruder it retreats with a fleetness that always surprises. It seldom leaves the ground, but runs from bush to bush in rapid zigzags. The nest, built in bushes or cactus patches, is almost invariably felted with filago, a downy little plant much prized by many desert birds as a nest lining.

Of the birds of prey, the spirited prairie falcon seems most typical of the desert. It nests on high cliffs, and the site of its home is easily detected during the nesting season by the piercing cries of the young and the equally wild, penetrating, distressful notes and daring, agitated flight of the parents. The large and powerful Western red-tailed hawk is also a cliff nester, and we not infrequently see its large stick nests mounted high on the steep canyon sides. Reptiles are a part of this hawk's bill-of-fare, and in summer I have seen the birds flying with large snakes in their talons. Turkey vultures are also resident in the desert area, and in autumn they at times gather in great numbers to roost in the cottonwood trees along the Mohave River. Along with the crows and ravens, they are always attracted by the carcasses of dead rabbits on the highways. No one has a better opportunity to study the habits of vultures than the observing motorist. When disturbed, the birds unfold their wings and take off with a vigorous spring; a few hurried flaps carry them to safety, and soon they are seen circling high in air, their wings set to the wind.

The intense and impressive stillness of the desert night is frequently broken by the wild, deep, measured notes—*whoo, hu-hoow, whoo, whoo*—of the horned owl. In the breeding season these notes are supplemented by a variety of other sounds, and if the birds happen to be perching on rocks near your desert camp you will be quite convinced that they are very noisy lovers. In spring the ear often catches other bird songs at night. I have repeatedly heard mocking birds, linnets, and desert sparrows bubble over in erratic song long after dark.

CHAPTER X

MAMMALIAN LIFE

THE desert's mammalian fauna is represented by thirty-six genera comprised of fully seventy-five species and subspecies. It is most interesting to note that at least two-thirds of the various mammals found on deserts belong to the order of rodents or gnawing animals. Of these rodents it has been the mice and their near relations that have been most successful, probably because they are, for the most part, burrowers, live on seeds and grasses, and are not dependent on ordinary sources of water for drink. They may be classed along with the hares and ground squirrels among the "savers." Few if any of them perspire, most of them pass scant amounts of urine, and many drink no water from the day of birth to the day of death, their dependence for water being placed wholly on the free water in their food and the water elaborated through the processes of metabolism. The average traveler is largely unaware of the presence of these animals, for they are active mostly at night. But if he is at all circumspect in his observations he will at least see the results of their active labors in the myriads of little holes and scratchings, to say nothing of the many dainty, lace-like track-patterns left in the sands to mark the countless journeys they make in search of seeds.

"One might," says Tristram, commenting on the rodents of the desert region adjacent to Palestine, "easily be accused of exaggerating in describing the countless number of holes and burrows in the regions which, for the greater part of the year, present features of utter desert. Sometimes for miles a region has the appearance of one vast warren of pygmy rabbit holes: yet for days, saving the bounding of a jerboa [a small, fawn-colored, jumping rodent] before one's horse, not another trace of rodent life is to be seen."

In the sand dunes, where digging is easy, almost every strong-rooted bush and tree has its kangaroo rat holes with well-beaten runways leading in all directions to the feeding-grounds. If the sands have been long undisturbed by winds they may contain many visible records of the merry waltzings and spirited hops and quarrels these animals engage in during the nocturnal hours.

One traveling over sand thickly occupied by kangaroo rats is certain to find himself all of a sudden in a foolish and laughable situation, for while he walks the ground suddenly begins to give way beneath him as the ceilings of numerous burrows cave in, and he reels like a drunken man in an earthquake. Every step forward sends him into new ludicrous positions; he may even fall headlong and go sprawling on the earth. Just about the time he feels that he has reached solid ground, down he goes again and he begins to wonder if there is any end to the extensiveness of the honeycomb of underground passages. I once saw a pack burro venture into such a place; the animal became so frightened that it could never be induced to try it again; in fact, it was ever afterward suspicious of any ground that sounded hollow beneath.

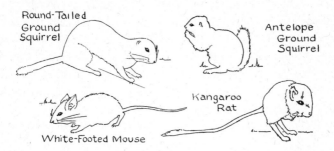

Round-Tailed Ground Squirrel

Antelope Ground Squirrel

Kangaroo Rat

White-Footed Mouse

If a tapping sound is made at the mouth of one of the numerous burrows, the animals within are likely to respond with a sound described by a well-known naturalist as having a churring or fluttering quality and resembling the noise of flying quail. It is probably a signal of alarm or note of challenge made with the hind feet striking repeatedly and rhythmically against the sands. Trade rats when annoyed respond in the same way over and over again.

There is scarcely a square mile of the desert, with the exception of the dry lakes, which does not have its share of white-footed mice.[1] These dainty, big-eared creatures are

[1] Dr. F. B. Sumner has made extensive studies of the way in which the colors of these mice vary with the colors of their environment. Like so many desert animals, the desert races of white-footed mice (*Peromyscus*) are usually much paler than those dwelling in more humid localities. This has commonly been interpreted as an instance of concealing coloration, evolved as a means of protection. There is doubtless some truth in this view. But Dr. Sumner and others offer reasons for believing that an arid climate may result in the loss of dark pigment in the skin, regardless of the color of the

found poking their noses into every possible rock cleft and beneath every succulent herb or bush. In winter they find their way into the settlers' cabins, stealing wads of cotton from the unprotected mattresses and getting into the supply cans unwittingly left open; in fact, they turn everything they explore or discover topsy-turvy and leave a sad mess of shredded papers, chewed rags, and tattered bags as evidence of their winter's occupation.

The grasshopper mice live such obscure and hidden lives that few people are ever aware of their existence. They are robust little fellows with short, thick tails and velvety fur. They live in burrows dug in the sand, and in these retreats lay up their small stores and build their nests of vegetable fibers. One of the chief items of their bill of fare is insects; grasshoppers and crickets are their favorites. The wide variety of other animal food, dead birds, lizards, and scorpions, is supplemented by many kinds of seeds. "At night,"

---

background on which the animal chances to dwell. He found, for instance, that a large collection of skins of a certain white-footed mouse, living upon an area of black lava in the Mohave Desert, displayed the characteristic pallor of desert races in general, and further he found that the color of these mice agreed very closely with that of a collection of the same species taken upon pale gray, buff, or pinkish rocks. Thus the precise correspondence between the color tones of the animal and those of its immediate background seems to have been overemphasized by some writers. On the other hand, the fact that pale races of mice occur on some of the isolated beaches of Florida, where there is high atmospheric humidity, is evidence that concealing coloration, achieved through natural selection, is one factor in the evolution of such races. Dr. Sumner expresses the belief that both of these agencies—the physiological effect of low atmospheric humidity and the selection of inconspicuous variations—have probably worked together toward producing the characteristic hues of desert mammals and birds.

says Vernon Bailey, "their presence is often made known by a firm, prolonged whistle, so sharp and shrill as to suggest the sound produced by some insect."

Harvest mice, the smallest of our desert mammals, live in the clumps of grass and weeds about the springs. They subsist chiefly on seeds. Their little ball-shaped nests are built above ground under cover of bushes and in grass tussocks. It is to these small beasts that we credit many of the tiny well-worn paths that run from place to place in the weed tangles. The color of the harvest mouse above is dark buffy-gray, that of the under parts light gray. If you would be sure of your identification you must have a specimen in hand and look for the deep groove running down the front of each upper incisor tooth.

The acquisitive habit, so necessary to the welfare of the animals living in an arid country where harvests are far between, is seen to perfection in the little spiny pocket mouse. Nature intended him to be a collector, for she gave him a pair of cheek pouches to serve as pockets in which to carry to his home underneath the rocks the winter stores of seeds. If you would know this sociable little rodent, establish your winter camp near a mountain with rocky slopes plunging steeply into the level sands of the desert floor. The chances are good that on the very first night in the flickering light of your campfire you will catch sight of the tiny, spiny-backed creature popping about on the ground and picking up crumbs from beneath your camp table. He is no bigger than a walnut, yet he can leap two or three feet with the ease of a kangaroo. Watch his tiny front feet move with the speed of a shuttle as they cram his little cheek pouches to fullness. No sooner has he made away with a load than he is back again, busier than ever. Above all things he is fond of butter, and I have had him more than once sit on my knee to nibble some from the end of my extended finger. You may talk about him as you please, but he completely ignores your presence; make the smallest movement of head, foot, or hand, however, and he is off in a flash. Continually menaced by the silent owls, by foxes, and by sidewinders, he is alert to every movement. He knows full well that his safety lies in reaching his hole among the rocks.

Wherever there are rocks and sticks you will come upon the trash-pile nests of the desert wood rats; old cabins, abandoned mine tunnels, caves, and brushy areas are alike popular resorts of these ambitious hoarders. Sharing equal honors in mischief with the white-footed mice, they are the despair of the prospector who lives in a shanty. All night long they are busy carrying to their nests anything they can seize; at making queer thumping and scratching noises they are prize-winners. Even in the open they are troublesome, for if you camp anywhere near their homes they are certain to pay you a visit before long and if they don't steal any of your effects they are sure to disturb you by their endless gnawings. I always inspect ironwood trees and mesquite thickets for nests before camping near them. The common wood rat over most of the Southeastern desert is the intermediate neotoma. Along the Colorado and Mohave rivers are subspecies of the dusky-footed brush rats, which build cone-shaped houses of dead sticks in brush and against tree trunks. Up in the desert mountains the neotomas often build, decorate, and protect their homes with freshly cut twigs of the juniper.

That little chipmunk-like creature with white tail held well over his back that scurried across the road and into the bushes as you approached was not a chipmunk as you suspected, but rather a miniature antelope ground squirrel.[2] You must expect to meet him almost everywhere you go. His scientific generic name, *Ammospermophilus,* means "lover of seed and sand," and his specific name, *leucurus,* has reference to his white tail. This little ground squirrel, or "ammo" as he is sometimes called, has a voice which for volume befits an animal ten times his size. The call is a long-continued, high-pitched, quavering trill and is most often heard in the mornings of spring. The young are absurd little midgets, "quiet as death," but interesting pets.

The antelope ground squirrel's nearest desert relative is the plain, light gray-coated, round-tailed ground squirrel. This rodent is largely confined to the areas of drifting sands. He, too, is a small fellow, who comes out in the daytime but is by no means so commonly seen as his relative with the loud stripes. He likes the succulent herbs, and in spring he eats until his little belly almost bursts. Though reputed to be a vegetarian, this squirrel sometimes feeds on his dead mates and on rabbits crushed by passing autos. He makes his burrow in the sands, being careful if possible to get it under some protecting root where the coyotes and kit foxes cannot easily dig him out.

The Western cotton rat is an animal seldom seen but often found by the trapper on the flats along the lower Colorado River. Evidence of his occupation of an area is seen in the little piles of cut willow twigs and nibbled tules on the sand under the food plants.

The burrowing activities of pocket gophers are marked

[2] The chipmunk's stripes run up to the point of the nose, while those of the ground squirrel end at the shoulder.

by the many fan-shaped mounds of loose earth which they push up from beneath the soil surface. The species occupying the delta soils of Imperial Valley is quite a different animal from the gopher of the opposite side of the Colorado River in Arizona and is also different from the very pallid Palm Springs gopher of the northwestern portion of the Colorado Desert. Because there are few places where the soil is sufficiently damp to work properly, gophers are necessarily rather rare desert animals. The Lone Pine pocket gopher is the only widespread species of the arid Mohave Desert. The Owens Lake gopher is restricted to the immediate vicinity of the vanishing salina, and several others are peculiar to isolated desert mountains.

Sonoran beavers were once plentiful along the Colorado River, but they are now scarce because of the continual trapping. The dam-building habit, so common to the northern animals, has been given up by them, perhaps, as Dr. Grinnell has suggested, because of the unsettled behavior of the river and because there is sufficient natural falling of the green cottonwood trees to supply the immediate needs of bark for food. Small stick houses, felled trees, and well-marked tracks are occasionally seen.

The black-tailed jack rabbit or desert hare is perhaps the most frequently noticed mammal of the desert. The little Arizona cottontail is there too, but seldom crosses our path. So long are the legs of the jack rabbits that the animals look on first sight almost like small coyotes. I never tire watching them bound gracefully away, and I enjoy equally well a sight of them peacefully feeding or jumping about under the brush or standing up on their haunches to get a broad view. And how clever they are at dropping their ears to protect the long appendages from injury when dashing under the thorny shrubs! Because of their habit of nibbling green crops, jack rabbits are the despair of the new settlers, and it is safe to say that these prolific animals have played an important rôle in keeping the desert the good wild place it was meant to be. Now and then the cacti feel the jack rabbit's sharp teeth and yield him an important supply of water.

The coyote is a perfectly typical wild dog. I sometimes feel that he has received, because of his howls, an almost undue amount of publicity. He speaks, it is true, in no uncertain sounds. His various wild calls to his mates as he goes out at evening time on the hunt are among the most fascinating of all the weird sounds that greet our ears. But the coyote has fallen on evil days. Relentlessly trapped and shot at by stupid gunners and killed by paid poison squads, he is no more king in his kingdom. We are genuinely sorry, because the coyote in his natural range is an animal worthy of our respect and admiration and a valuable destroyer of noxious rodents. This wild dog has a reputation of being a coward, yet he is in fact a ferocious carnivore that pursues his prey with daring and skill. He brings great cunning to bear when hard after his fleeting meals. If you do not believe it, ask the jack rabbits.

The kit fox or desert swift is decidedly the most handsome of the larger mammals of the region. He is at once so graceful and so beautifully furred that a man who traps one must feel like a scoundrel for having brought misery and death to so fine an animal. Shy and timid in the daytime, he becomes bold at night, or perhaps we should say unsuspicious, and sometimes steals into our camp to pick up the scraps we always throw out to attract the wild creatures.

The kangaroo rats of the dunes hold him no friend of theirs, for he is always appearing at the wrong time, breaking up their carnivals of play, and gobbling up the luckless ones for his midnight meal. Once plentiful, this splendid little fox is now fast disappearing over most of the desert area. Every autumn scores of shiftless families of trappers, thinking only of the few dollars they can get and possessing no regard for the welfare of the country's wild life, run long steel-trap lines, many of them fully 200 miles long, and remain until late in the spring killing off every animal that can be baited. They leave the whole country a wreck in so far as wild life is concerned. Their activities should certainly be curbed.

The kit fox's nearest kin in the desert area is the Arizona gray fox, a much larger animal of decidedly darker color. He is rather prone to stay in the hills and rocky canyons and leave the valleys and sandy flats to his smaller neighbor. On dark, cloudy days he may be out in the daytime a bit, but his regular hours for the hunt begin at dusk and last until dawn. Unsuspicious and often foolish, he stands small chance against the wiles of his human persecutors.

The little spotted skunk is as handsome a beast as we see on the desert and in spite of his regrettable habit of emitting an abominable-smelling fluid when he thinks his rights are invaded we give him almost first place among our favorite carnivores. He is really quite exemplary at minding his own business. By faithfully making his rounds over a wide area every night in search of wild mice and insects he gets a good living from the rocky country he inhabits. We regret that in his quest for something to eat he sometimes sets his paw in a trap. The hydrophobia skunk, as he is sometimes called, is no more guilty as a carrier of rabies than the coyote or any other desert animal. Skunks walk about on the palms of their hands and the soles of their little black feet after the fashion of bears. No kitten is more playful or dexterous with its paws. The big Arizona striped skunk is confined to the thickets along the Colorado River, kept there because of its daily need for water.

The desert has its own raccoon. Along waterways in the Imperial Valley and along sloughs, ponds, and channels of the Colorado River occurs the pallid coon. He lives principally on the unfortunate fish left by the overflows and on such small mammals, frogs, and insects as he can get on the muddy margins of the pools. Ring-tailed cats belonging to the same animal family (*Procyonidae*) are rare inhabitants of our desert areas.

It is yet possible now and then to see a badger. Though always persecuted by man, who ought to be his best friend, the badger has managed to survive in some of the more remote, unsettled basins. Squat of form and awkward in gait, he always strikes me as the queerest looking animal I meet on my travels. The badger's home is a deep hole in the ground, placed, if possible, under the protecting roots of some sturdy shrub. His strong, well-clawed limbs enable him to do the excavating in a hurry once he starts the task. A favorite sport of the cattlemen is to lasso the badger, let him get into his hole, and try to pull him out. The appetite of this carnivore is enormous. "Almost the whole life of the badger," says Vernon Bailey, "is spent in digging out the various rodents that constitute his food. It requires two or three fat ground squirrels, or a few gophers and a dozen mice, every day, to keep a badger in good condition."

In their hunting expeditions, wildcats wander widely and

are always bobbing up in the most unexpected places. When in their new coat of winter fur they are good-looking animals, but by the end of winter the coat of gray, brown, and black is ragged and dirty. Wildcats hunt both by night and by day, and in their excursions through the brush they catch birds, rabbits, and other small mammals. The desert lynxes show the same tendency toward paleness of color found in so many desert animals. I cannot believe that pallor of coat originated in this animal as a protective character, for the wildcat has few natural enemies other than man.

Black-tailed deer wander far out over the arid mountains in the winter and sometimes descend into the warm desert valleys where there are springs. In late autumn, deer in numbers from the cold, high Sierra make the long journey across Owens Valley to the Death Valley region where they can enjoy a warm winter. I have several times in winter found them seeking water at springs in the barren mountains east of the Salton Sea. In years past the big-eared burro deer was found along the Colorado River bottoms, but I have heard of only one small group in recent years. It has gone the way of the antelope, which was once plentiful, especially on the mesas of the Mohave Desert.

I have already dwelt at length in my former book, *Denizens of the Desert,* on the habits of the noble desert bighorn, and I shall let the reader seek more information about him there. It is a shame that the doom of this fine animal is written. He has held his own against the hunters longer than we had expected. Go to his haunts, reader; see him; but please be half a man and do not shoot! In spite of some so-called "official reports" in which the sheep are numbered by several thousands, I am constrained to affirm there are no more than five or six hundred sheep left in all the desert ranges of California. If they were even one-half as plentiful as some selfish interests proclaim them to be, it would be easy to see sheep everywhere. Most of those who observe carefully do well to see a few in two or three months or even in as many years.

On wide elastic wings millions of bats emerge silently from the deep rock crevices and old mines at early dusk. They come out with empty stomachs and soon are wheeling about, hawking for insects. Often on moonlight nights I have lain awake and have watched them swinging their way back and forth above my head.

The first bat to appear after dark is a little *Pipistrellus*. It is a bat of swift and erratic flight, flying high against the sky, but it may sometimes be seen abroad before sunset and in the morning after sunrise. Later in the evening the little buff-colored pallid bat comes forth and begins flying in low zigzag manner above the low bushes, but seldom appears above the sky-line.

The shrill and cicada-like note of the pale lump-nosed bat is often heard all through the night. This bat is called the burro bat by the miners because of its long ears and also the lump-nosed bat because of the peculiar glandular swelling on the sides of its nose. It roosts in the daytime in tunnels and caves throughout the desert area.

The spotted bat belongs to a genus (*Eudermia*) confined wholly to southwestern United States. It was once described by a desert resident as a large bat "with ears like a jackass and a white stripe on each shoulder." He might well have mentioned in addition the white patch on its rump and its remarkably furless, parchment-like wings and tail membrane.

CHAPTER XI

THE ABORIGINES OF THE DESERT

BY MALCOLM J. ROGERS

IT IS only in comparatively recent times that man through the advancement of science has mastered nature to the extent of residing not only where he pleases but, in a degree, how he pleases. With primitive man the obverse obtained, especially in those two most inimical environments, the arid and the polar regions of the earth. Strive as he might in an unfavorable habitat, man's cultural attainments and everyday life were determined almost exclusively by this environment. Comparative studies of the ethnology of desert peoples the world over have disclosed remarkable parallelisms in their histories, for which like conditions are held responsible.

If those readers to whom the American desert is as yet unknown will bear in mind its nature as set forth in this and other works, they will acquire more easily an understanding of its native peoples, their problems, and how they met them. They will view their simple achievements not with disdain but rather with admiration for the ingenuity displayed in the eternal combat with one of the world's worst deserts.

The first Europeans to visit this region found the desert in the possession of various divisions of two great native stocks, the Yuman and the Shoshonean. Their respective sections roughly paralleled the Colorado River, with the former occupying the river basin and the latter the western fringe of the desert. Both stocks, near their southern extensions, had off-shoots that reached the Pacific Coast but in a territory with which we are not concerned.

This historical arrangement, as well as being more or less consonant with the prehistoric grouping, is also indicative of the pathways these ancient Americans followed to the south out of the Great Basin into southern California. The Yumans preceded their Shoshonean neighbors by many hundreds of years in the region, and in early times occupied much of the desert lands that were later ceded to the Shoshoneans. The Yumans gave way, especially on their northwestern flank, withdrawing to the valley of the Colorado, until in historic times the Mohave Desert had fallen almost entirely into the hands of the Shoshoneans. This relinquishment, although due in part to warfare, was brought about mainly by adverse climatic and physiographic changes that will be spoken of later, changes that made the Yumans only too glad to remove to better lands.

Those who are familiar with the numerous vestiges of former Indian camps and villages that are to be met with throughout the Mohave and Colorado deserts are immediately impressed with the problem of their presence. Because these sites are often without a water supply and are usually surrounded by a scanty flora and an even scantier fauna, it seems incredible that men once eked out a living in such places. The problem, however, yields, as others have done, to patient investigation. If we but draw upon and correlate the findings in such sciences as geology, climatology, and botany, the mystery is no longer a mystery.

Although the natural sciences have shown that the inception of the California deserts was some twenty thousand years ago at the end of the geological period known as the Pleistocene, they also disclose that the intensity of the aridity has been far from constant. There are many evidential factors in the region which would indicate that several periods of comparative wetness intervened in the general progression toward maximum aridity which exists today. Even in historic times many desert springs and waterholes have disappeared. Bearing such conditions in mind, we must visualize a mobility in human occupation in the desert and must recognize that not all archaeological sites are of the same age. In a way, their respective presences in specific regions are a reflection of favorable ecological conditions of bygone periods.

At least one section of this area, in so far as it concerns a favorable habitat for man, has always been immune to climatic fluctuations: that section is the valley of the Colorado River. Here was not only a permanent water supply but also an annual growth of edible native plant foods. The river provided several species of fish and its environs much game in the way of birds and animals. After the flood-waters of early summer had receded, the muddy flood-plain of the Colorado was available for a crude form of agriculture; on it the various river tribes planted corn, squash, melons, and possibly beans. It was in this region that the greatest population and most constant occupation was maintained; it must be regarded as the culture-center of the desert tribes, although the germ of the culture was derived from southern Arizona in an earlier time. Here, too, archaeological research has yielded the earliest evidence of man in the area with which we are concerned.

In the desert interior, Indian settlements, with but few exceptions, were small and rather evenly distributed. These exceptions of relatively dense occupation were about the shores of both permanent and intermittent fresh-water lakes. These post-Pleistocene permanent lakes have been extinct for some hundreds of years, and are now spoken of as dry lakes or sinks. From the nature and amount of archaeological material occurring on the strands of these fossil lakes, several facts may be determined: such as, what tribes lived there, when they did so, and what their everyday life was like.

In the north central part of San Bernardino County, in the vicinity of the great Mohave Sink into which the Mohave River now empties intermittently and only during a season of exceptional run-off, was once a chain of fresh-water lakes. Wave terraces and deposits of tufa on rocky promontories record the former presence and extent of these lakes of the desert. About their margins the Mohave Indians lived for hundreds of years. From their waters they took some fish and quantities of fresh-water mussels. In the surrounding desert sands, heaps of charred mussel-shells, incongruously conspicuous, record many an ancient feast. During these times it was possible to supplement the natural food supply by practicing agriculture about the mouth of the Mohave River.

At present it is impossible to state definitely when or how long such idyllic conditions prevailed in the Mohave, but archaeological studies would indicate that the Mohaves held this territory more or less continuously from the tenth to the sixteenth centuries and probably even earlier. At the end of this period, they withdrew to join the River Mohaves on the Colorado, forced out undoubtedly by increasing aridity and by warfare with Shoshonean migrants, principally Cheme-huevi from the north. In 1776, Garces, the Spanish missionary and the first European to cross the Mohave, found the latter people in possession of the region, undesirable as it was.

The Chemehuevi, perhaps the most miserable Indians in the West, were undoubtedly victims of their environment. With the more advanced Shoshonean tribes holding the western rim of the desert and the Yumans of the Colorado River basin hemming them in on the east, the Chemehuevi were compelled to wander about in small groups on the Mohave Desert. Their continual struggle to circumvent starvation left them no time to settle in towns and to build up a material culture; consequently they came and went, leaving but few evidences of their presence. They were peculiarly addicted to pecking various symbols and animal portraits on the smooth black rocks of the desert. These numerous petroglyphs are often the sole evidence of their former presence in certain regions. Today their descendants are to be found on a reservation near Parker on the Colorado, between the reservations of their old enemies, the Mohaves and the Yumas.

In the center of the Colorado Desert, and approximately at the same time as the last lake in the Mohave Sink, Lake Cahuilla, the greatest lake of all, existed. This great fresh-water body, with a shore line of 250 miles, came into being

through the sudden shifting of the course of the Colorado
River. The normal drainage of the river into the Gulf of
California then as well as now depended on an unobstructed
channel. As nearly as can be determined through geological
evidence, about 900 A.D. the deltaic cone silted to such a
height that the river slipped off the obstruction to the west,
then turned north, and became entrapped in the great
Salton Basin depression. Almost at once a miraculous oasis
was thus created where arid alkaline flats had persisted
for ages. With water, vegetation springs forth like magic
in the warm desert lands. Lake Cahuilla almost immediately
became fringed with tule, arrowweed, and willows, and
later with mesquite and even a few palms, the dead stumps
of which are sometimes met with along the now dry strand.
The waters of the lake teemed with fish and on its surface
swarms of aquatic birds settled down.

The Indians in the lower end of the Colorado River basin
were quick to take advantage of this desert paradise, and
there was undoubtedly a rapid exodus from the river to the
lake. The Yumans soon spread completely around this huge
lake that provided such a tempting environment. For some
years the Colorado waters maintained the lake at a general
level with but few fluctuations, but during one of the high-
level phases all the Indian villages on a certain contour
were inundated for a long period. A record of this ancient
flood has been found in the travertine deposits on the
abandoned house-stones and implements. Afterward the
lake shrank down to sea-level, where it maintained itself
long enough to cut another distinct terrace. The natives
moved down to the new shore-line, but shortly afterward
abandoned the lake forever. During the lake's last phase,

the Colorado flowed into it so intermittently that its waters became undrinkable owing to the concentration of soluble salts. In some sections, and especially about the San Felipe Hills where the old strands are well preserved, as many as four village-sites may be discerned, on as many different terraces, within a distance of two miles. It is thought that Lake Cahuilla disappeared completely about 1500 A.D.

Today one may walk for miles on the fossil strands of this lake and be continually in sight of potsherds, patches of burnt fish-bone, and other habitational débris. It is difficult now to gaze off over the miles of arid, sandy wastes and comprehend that here once lived thousands of people in a land of plenty. There are Indians yet alive who have verbally perpetuated their ancestors' tales of the time when much of the desert was under water. The disappearance of Lake Cahuilla compelled the tribes on the east shore to move back to the Colorado River and those on the west shore to move into the mountains of San Diego County.

Before leaving the subject it is well to consider the so-called "fish-traps" of the Coachella Valley, located below the high terrace of Lake Cahuilla on the bowlder talus of the Santa Rosa Mountains. They are in the form of circular pits, and were built in the stony talus by throwing out a quantity of the loose stones to form a crater-like structure. As fish-traps they would not be effective in a tideless sea, and Indian informants have often proclaimed them for what they were—houses—yet the misnomer persists. In other parts of the Salton Basin, such as at the foot of Fish Creek Mountain, I have found them even above the highest lake terrace and invariably associated with potsherds, charcoal, and fishbone.

To the imaginative traveler in every realm, certain inevitable questions arise to perplex the mind. Are the historical natives the aboriginal inhabitants, or were they preceded in the region by other peoples, and if so, how long ago? In some places where archaeological material is plentiful and, what is more important, occurs under the proper conditions for the specialist to interpret, such questions are not difficult to answer. Our region, however, does not provide these ideal conditions. It is one in which neither the native customs nor the elements were conducive to the preservation of evidence. All of the desert peoples cremated their dead, burned their houses, and destroyed the personal effects of the deceased. This, coupled with the terrific erosion occasioned by cloudbursts, has left little evidence for a reconstruction of the past.

In the valley of the Colorado River not even the village sites of the historic tribes have been preserved. They were built on the low islands and on the flood-plain where the annual floods of this great river have either swept them away or buried them under tons of silt. The Colorado floods annually in the early summer for a short period, and it was the custom of the Indians to retire to the highlands each year at this time to await the recession of the high waters. This seems at first glance an impractical way of living, yet it was imperative. In the entire desert region the cottonwood and willow forests of the river-bottom afford the only shelter, so necessary from the terrific heat of the sun. Then, too, their simple brush and pole houses were easily rebuilt.

On the stony mesas that are so typical of much of the Colorado Desert, and especially of the immediate terraces of the Colorado River basin, occur the only manifestations of a possible prior people. On such lands are found thousands of small circular clearings that probably mark the sites of ancient wikiups. No material remnants, such as potsherds and stone tools of the kind indicative of the Yuman civilization, are to be found near them. In fact nothing but the crudest stone scrapers are associated with these house sites. Since their manufacture, the scrapers have gathered a coating of the lustrous dark patina so characteristic of most of the desert rocks. If the time-rate of deposition of this desert varnish were known, their antiquity might be set, but it is not. That the tools are ancient is apparent when one compares them with the fresh, unoxidized surfaces of Yuman implements.

In proximity to the house-circles of these early inhabitants occur figures of huge dimensions laid out in the flat gravel surfaces of the mesas. Both by raking the surface gravels into lines and by clearing them in definite areas, geometrical figures were constructed on so large a scale that they may be visualized only by aerial photography. Such work is unique in America, so far as I know. In later times, the Yuman Indians occasionally built both human and animal figures by means of the same technique. These later structures are readily distinguished by their fresher appearance and by the fact that they are sometimes superimposed on the older figures. Although by far the greater number of these figures are concentrated in the valley of the Colorado River in the vicinity of Blythe, a few are to be found about the margins of the Salton Basin and the Laguna Salada Basin in Lower California. As all these remains that indicate archaeological antiquity occur within the Yuman territory, they may well be the creations of their progenitors, for the Yumans seem to have been established in the region at an early date.

The greatest material manifestation of aboriginal effort, however, is to be encountered in the ancient turquoise mines in the north-central part of the Mohave Desert. Many years before the Mohaves settled in the region, a more cultured people who lived in southern Nevada and were related to the Puebloans discovered these deposits and periodically visited them to procure the blue-green stone that was as precious to them as gold is to us. These turquoise deposits are scattered over a considerable area, yet the Puebloans seem to have found them all, for modern prospectors say that they have never found an unworked outcropping. In the Shadow Mountains, where many of the turquoise-bearing porphyry veins are under a deep overburden, the Indians were compelled to dig deep pits to the bedrock and break up the hard porphyry with stone picks and mauls, after which the débris was gathered by hand and carried out in baskets. It is most impressive to perceive the extent and number of these old workings, in view of the crude methods and tools employed. A few of the larger pits measure twenty feet in diameter and twelve feet in depth.

In the northern half of the Mohave Desert, extending from the Owens River east to the Colorado River, is an area that probably contains more Indian picture writings than any equal area in the United States. This region contains at least thirty thousand petroglyphs, or incised rock drawings. Several of the isolated groups exhibit as many as five hundred detached glyphs, and at the Piute Creek site they appear on both sides of the canyon for a distance of two miles. This group contains nearly eight hundred of these interesting records of primitive art.

Pictographs, or rock paintings, are exceedingly scarce in the Mohave, and the same is true of the Colorado Desert, where petrography[1] is less common. This predominance of incised drawings over painted ones is imposed by nature and is not a matter of human preference, for the dark coating of desert rocks does not provide a background suitable for the dull earth-pigments used in such work. Pictographs are almost entirely confined to the light-colored granitic mountains that form the western margin of the California desert.

An intensive and protracted study of this subject has disclosed several things. The petroglyphs were made not only by different tribes but at different periods. Certain motifs are noticeably restricted to specific areas, while other motifs are common to the entire area. The latter types are usually of zoic form, as one would expect, whereas the more specialized geometrical figures have the most restricted distribution.

Naturally the purpose and meaning of the symbols employed interest people mostly. There is widespread belief that they were placed where they were to direct the bewildered aborigine to water, to mineral resources, or to the next settlement. As one usually has to find such accommodations first in order to find the glyphs, the traveler's-guide theory need not be considered. In fact, the motive for most of this work is still operative today. Witness how few persons can resist placing their names or initials in conspicuous

---

[1] Petrography is here used as a generic term to include both incised and painted drawings on rocks.

places or utilizing an idle hour in exercising their sketching ability on the nearest medium. The Indian responded to the same impulse by recording his name, his totem, or his clan's name in rebus. Although most of the desert petrography may be accounted for in this manner, there is another type in the Shoshonean territory of southern California with a different origin. This type comprises an elaborate group of painted geometrical forms. They were constructed either by medicine men or initiates under their guidance, and are of a ceremonial nature.

Perhaps the most imposing of all the petroglyph sites is the one in Grapevine Canyon in the Spirit Mountains. These were the sacred mountains of Yuman mythology, and high on their eastern flank Grapevine Canyon breaks out through a massive portal of russet-brown granite into a small basin. The walls, rising almost vertically for over one hundred feet on either side of the canyon floor, from top to bottom are covered with glyphs of varying age and style. The earliest are of considerable antiquity, for several physiographic changes have occurred since they were traced: first, the basin into which the canyon opens filled up with alluvium to a depth of twenty feet; then, at a later period, it was eroded out to bedrock. This last action scoured the sides of the portal enough to obliterate most of the lower figures. Many above this level have been nearly effaced by a coating of oxides; such old figures often have later ones superimposed on them.

Although it has been pointed out that most of the petrography of the region is in the vicinity of watering-places, camps, and village sites, some is to be found where no such associations are apparent. It is noticeable, however, that the aberrant sites are usually located in passes or at the mouths of canyons through which Indian trails passed.

These ancient highways are imposing in number, in extent, and in degree of preservation. Several of the more important ones are worth considering in view of the purpose they served. The main north-south trails on both banks of the Colorado arrest the attention because of their length, being traceable from Nevada down the river to Mexico; but it is the east-and-west trade trails that are the most interesting. The most important and probably most ancient trail of this nature crossed the Mohave Desert in the latitude of the Mohave Sink; beginning somewhere in northern Arizona, it crossed the desert, and ended at the west on the Pacific Coast. Over this route the Mohaves for hundreds of years brought sea-shells to trade with the Pueblos of Arizona for pottery and pigments. Early white explorers and military expeditions often followed this route in later days.

Through the Colorado Desert ran the second great east-and-west trail, that likewise began in Arizona, in the southern part on the Gila River. It crossed the Colorado River in the vicinity of Palo Verde and from here struck off across the desert to the northwest, traversing the length of Coachella Valley and joining the Mohave Trail near San Bernardino. Along the main trails, desert Indians practiced the peculiar custom of depositing small stones in piles to indicate that they had made one of these long treks. (See headpiece for chapter xvi.) In time many of the piles grew to considerable size. The piles usually occur in groups, a fact that may be explained by assuming that each clan constructed a separate pile. There is also some evidence that not all such structures were merely for the purpose of recording journeys but were the outgrowth of a ritual practice. In such piles the travelers seem to have sacrificed a portion of whatever they were carrying in an effort to effect a successful journey by appeasing some spirit or deity. They were particular either to break or to burn all offerings before depositing them.

Desert trail-markers kept to the stony mesas wherever it was feasible, for Indians always avoided walking in sand if possible. Long trail sections are still intact, and as fresh as in the days when they were used constantly. Today over the dark malpais lands of the Colorado Desert these narrow, cleared pathways wind their tortuous ways, enduring records of ancient travel.

CHAPTER XII

BOTANICAL ASPECTS OF
ARID REGIONS

THE remarkable vegetation of the desert areas of the world has received the attentive study of many botanists. Evidence of an early active interest in the flora of arid America is found in the reports of the explorers who traveled over the West country in connection with various military and railway expeditions undertaken in the first three-quarters of the nineteenth century. In the appendices of the often bulky volumes we find beautifully wrought illustrations of the bizarre plants which pleased the eyes of such intrepid botanist-explorers as John C. Frémont, John Torrey, and Dr. Edward Palmer. The accounts of the journeys of these men form some of the most fascinating narratives in American literature; they verily make one travel-hungry. Few writings of the present are as vigorous or as refreshing in their descriptions of localities and of plants growing there.

The desert's floral season is, on the whole, a short one, a show of wild beauty that lasts at best but six weeks or three months, from February through April and May. In ordinary years when winter and early spring rains are scarce,

130

the annual flowering plants are few, and inasmuch as they are in no particular way adapted to endure shortage of water they wilt and die a few weeks after they have sprung, as if by magic, from the barren earth. As though trying to make up for this scant contribution to beauty, every few years comes an abundance of rain and there results such a wealth of blossoms that almost every foot of sand or rocky soil is hidden beneath a blanket of flowers.

Gilias, primroses, phacelias, and various species of wild buckwheats and composites are among the commonest and most widely distributed of the annual plants. Where seeds of the previous seasons have lodged in the sands about the bases of the shrubs, myriads of these and other short-lived flowers spring up and form soft, flowery cushions whose appearance of luxuriance is much heightened by the inter-mingling growths of small grasses. In late spring the west-ern rim of the Mohave Desert is aglow with fields of Ken-nedy's mariposa (*Calochortus kennedyi*), a lily with large orange-chrome petals and contrasting purple anthers. When it comes out in force on the gravelly mesas and rocky hills, the Mohave aster (*Aster abatus*), with broad lilac-colored flowers on tall, graceful stems, presents an equally striking spectacle. In the desert's interior we see great stretches covered with carpets of short-statured, royal-purple lupines (*Lupinus odoratus*), or fields stippled lemon and green with countless stalks of caulanthus (*C. inflatus*), the squaw's cabbage of the Indians and the pioneers.

On the Colorado Desert the best shows of color are made by the pink verbenas, golden encelias (*Geraea canescens*), and great white primroses (*Oenothera detoides*). The tips of the stout stems of the dying primroses meet to form curious "baskets" which long remain as strange decorations on the sun-drenched sands. This habit of basket formation, as yet unexplained, is shared by a number of other desert plants.

Volcanic soils and those of the flats surrounding many of the dry-type dry lakes seem unusually well suited to the needs of many kinds of wild buckwheats and chorizanthes, and among the spectacular sights of early summer are the colorful stretches of blossoming plants. As they come to maturity, the stems turn a warm chestnut red, and frequently not only the dry· lake margins but whole valley floors and their bordering detrital fans glow with ruddy color.

Careful estimates based on check lists reveal the fact that the California deserts support no less than seven hundred species of flowering plants. What a contrast is this to the monotonous and meager flora of the Old World deserts! Because of the uniformity of land surface and the lack of varied environment there, the few genera and species of plants are distributed with little interruption from the Sahara's far western limits to the mid-region of Turkestan.

The flora of much of the United States and Canada has many features in common with that of Europe and Asia, and this fact is taken as almost certain evidence of the former existence of a land bridge between Eurasia and North America. It is indeed possible that from Europe and Asia the ancestors of a good proportion of our northern flora were acquired. The botanists tell us that the deserts of North America have derived their plant genera from a very different source. The genera so common in the north are here replaced by such odd, xerophilous plants as the yuccas, agaves, ocotillos, and cacti, all plants of strictly American distribution that were probably first developed on the great arid Sonoran plateau of Mexico. It was near the end of the glacial epoch and the beginning of the development of arid conditions in California that these plants of the Mexican realm pushed northward and gave us this most unique flora. The deserts of southern Arizona and of the Salton Sea area show this invasion of the Mexican element much more strongly than the deserts of the Great Basin region.

It is now known that many desert plants, among them the hardy desert shrubs, are great drinkers and almost reckless spenders of water when they can get it. In fact, in many cases they appear to be more improvident with their water supply than plants of humid regions. In general it may be said that the chief distinction between desert plants and those of moister lands lies not, as we so often are led to believe, in their ability to get along with scant amounts of water but in their power to endure long-continued wilting and to recover from it unharmed when the rains come again. Creosote bushes near Bagdad on the Mohave Desert stood through the long drought of 1909–1912 when for thirty-two months not a drop of precipitation was recorded and the interval between effective rains was still longer. They came to the end of the dry period with scarcely a leaf left—as miserable a lot of plants as one ever saw. How they ever became green again is little short of a mystery.

Desert plants commonly exhibit certain peculiar structural characters such as thorns and leathery leaves which are protected against evaporation by hairs, resiny coats, reduced surface, and sunken stomata. Such adaptations were long thought to be a reaction to the hot, dry atmosphere and the meager water supply at the root. When plant physiologists observed that plants of bogs and salt marshes show these same modifications it was concluded that, though the roots were planted in wet earth, they suffered from lack of water even as the desert plants did. These marsh plants, they said, were subjected to "physiological drought," i.e., water was "considered not readily available to the plant on account of the high osmotic pressure of salt solutions, bad aëration in marshes, and bog toxins." But this explanation, they soon discovered, was not adequate. Recent studies carried on by Dr. Kurt Mothes of Germany point to the possibility that both desert and marsh and bog plants produce their similar, peculiar structures because of the lack of nitrogen in the soil.

For those seeking an easy means of identifying the desert flowers, trees, and shrubs, I have made drawings of the commoner species. Unfortunately, many of the plants have had no common or English names assigned to them and we have to be content with the scientific nomen. Unless otherwise stated, all of the illustrations show the plants reduced to one-half natural size. For the identification of plants not shown here, the reader is referred to *A Manual of the Flowering Plants of California,* by Dr. W. L. Jepson, and the forthcoming *Manual of Southern California Botany,* by Dr. Philip A. Munz.

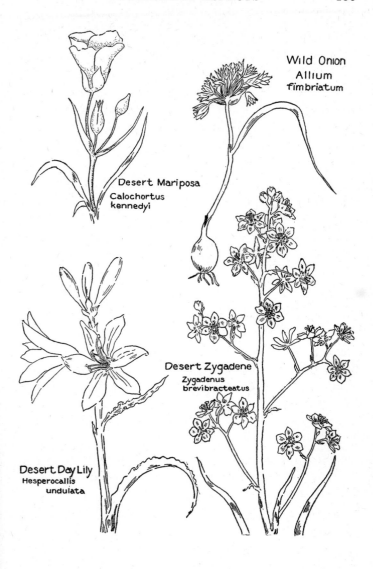

Desert Mariposa
Calochortus
kennedyi

Wild Onion
Allium
fimbriatum

Desert Zygadene
Zygadenus
brevibracteatus

Desert Day Lily
Hesperocallis
undulata

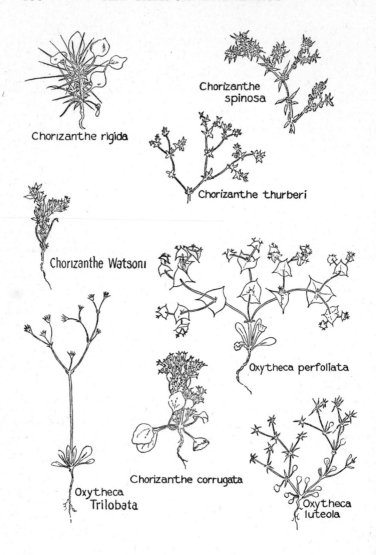

Chorizanthe rigida

Chorizanthe spinosa

Chorizanthe thurberi

Chorizanthe Watsoni

Chorizanthe corrugata

Oxytheca perfollata

Oxytheca Trilobata

Oxytheca luteola

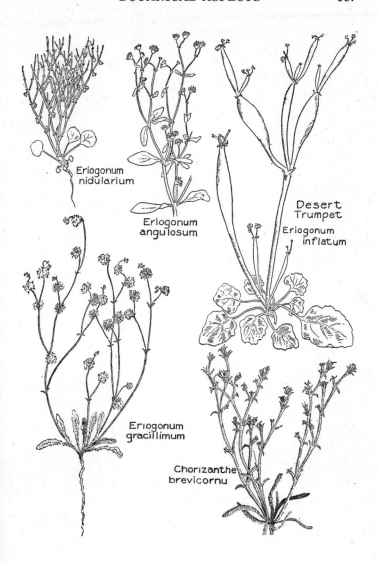

Eriogonum
nidularium

Eriogonum
angulosum

Desert
Trumpet
Eriogonum
inflatum

Eriogonum
gracillimum

Chorizanthe
brevicornu

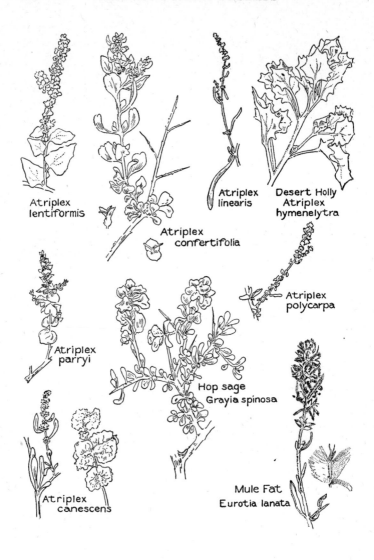

Atriplex
lentiformis

Atriplex
confertifolia

Atriplex
linearis

Desert Holly
Atriplex
hymenelytra

Atriplex
parryi

Atriplex
polycarpa

Hop sage
Grayia spinosa

Atriplex
canescens

Mule Fat
Eurotia lanata

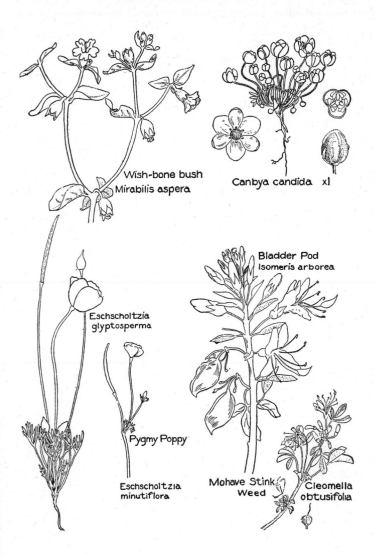

Wish-bone bush
Mirabilis aspera

Canbya candida   x1

Bladder Pod
Isomeris arborea

Eschscholtzia
glyptosperma

Pygmy Poppy

Eschscholtzia
minutiflora

Mohave Stink
Weed

Cleomella
obtusifolia

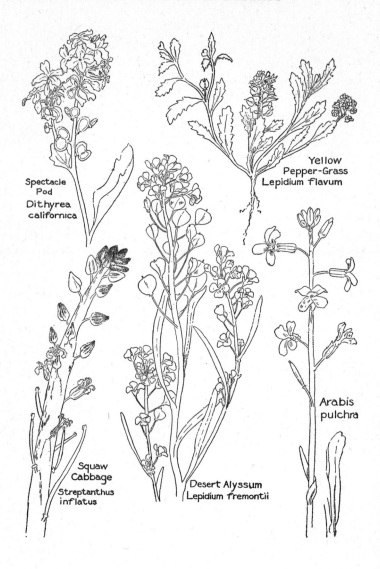

Spectacle
Pod
Dithyrea
californica

Yellow
Pepper-Grass
Lepidium flavum

Squaw
Cabbage
Streptanthus
inflatus

Desert Alyssum
Lepidium fremontii

Arabis
pulchra

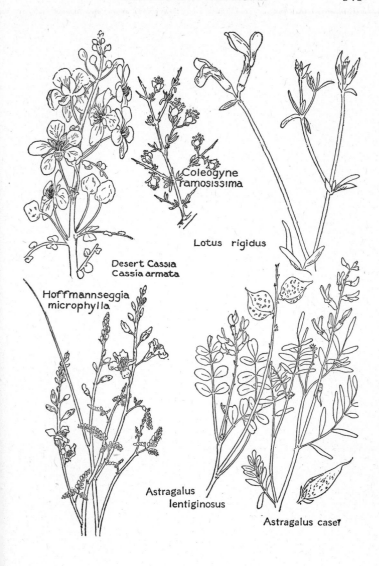

Coleogyne
ramosissima

Lotus rigidus

Desert Cassia
Cassia armata

Hoffmannseggia
microphylla

Astragalus
lentiginosus

Astragalus casei

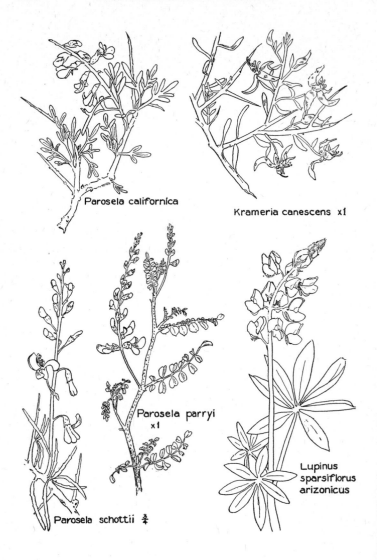

Parosela californica

Krameria canescens x1

Parosela parryi
x1

Parosela schottii ¾

Lupinus
sparsiflorus
arizonicus

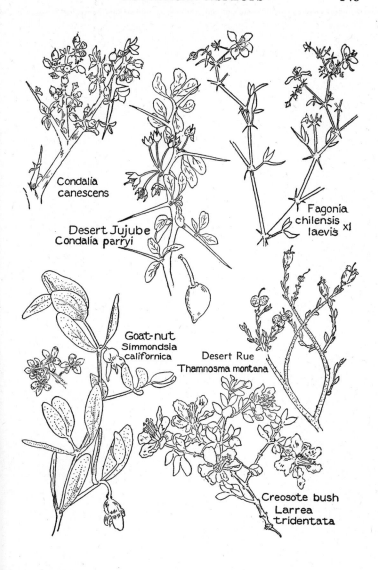

Condalia
canescens

Desert Jujube
Condalia parryi

Fagonia
chilensis
laevis x1

Goat-nut
Simmondsia
californica

Desert Rue
Thamnosma montana

Creosote bush
Larrea
tridentata

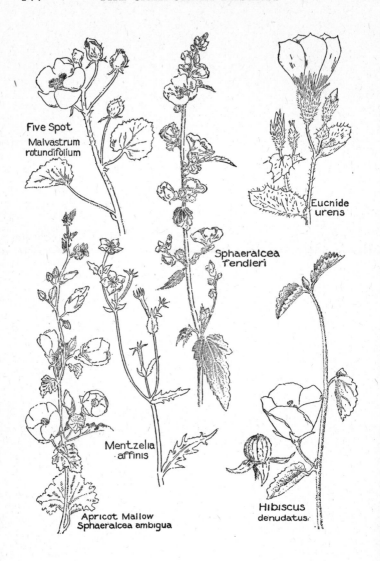

Five Spot
Malvastrum
rotundifolium

Eucnide
urens

Sphaeralcea
Fendleri

Mentzelia
affinis

Apricot Mallow
Sphaeralcea ambigua

Hibiscus
denudatus

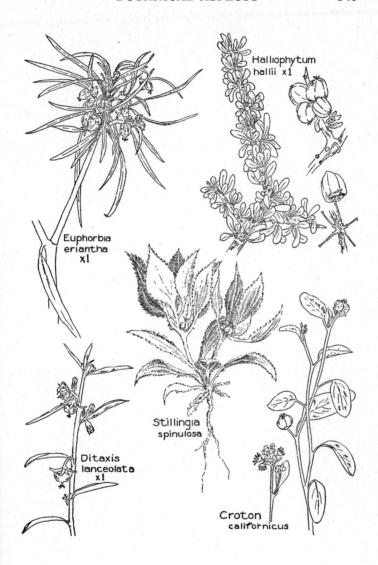

Euphorbia
eriantha
x1

Halliophytum
hallii x1

Stillingia
spinulosa

Ditaxis
lanceolata
x1

Croton
californicus

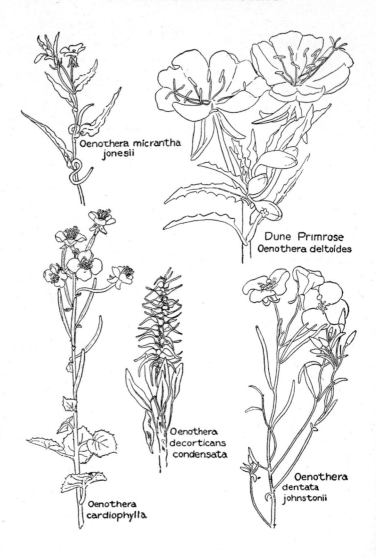

Oenothera micrantha jonesii

Dune Primrose
Oenothera deltoides

Oenothera decorticans condensata

Oenothera cardiophylla

Oenothera dentata johnstonii

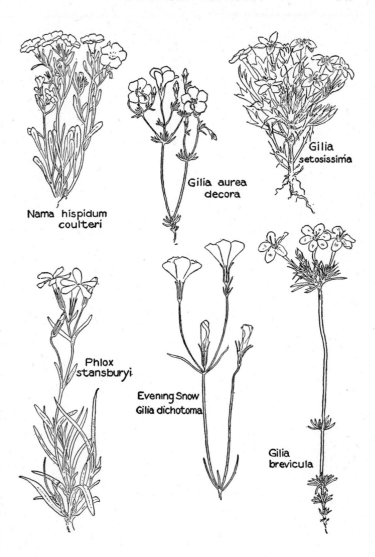

Nama hispidum
coulteri

Gilia aurea
decora

Gilia
setosissima

Phlox
stansburyi

Evening Snow
Gilia dichotoma

Gilia
brevicula

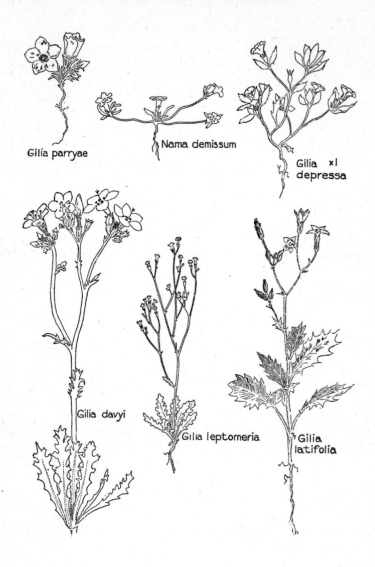

Gilia parryae

Nama demissum

Gilia x1
depressa

Gilia davyi

Gilia leptomeria

Gilia
latifolia

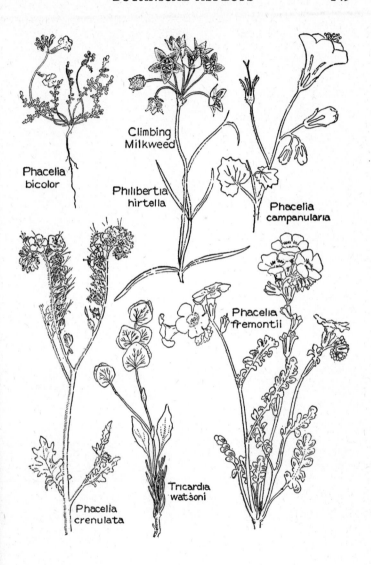

Phacelia
bicolor

Climbing
Milkweed

Philibertia
hirtella

Phacelia
campanularia

Phacelia
fremontii

Phacelia
crenulata

Tricardia
watsoni

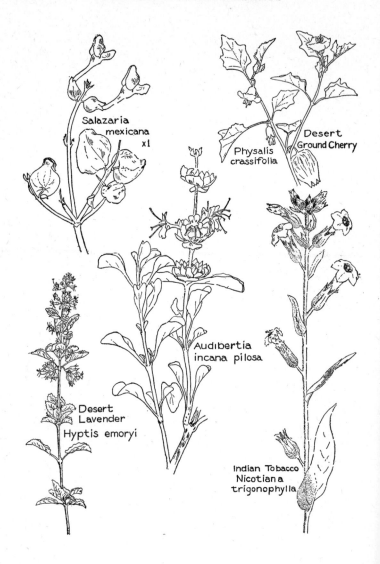

Salazaria
mexicana
x1

Physalis
crassifolia

Desert
Ground Cherry

Audibertia
incana pilosa

Desert
Lavender

Hyptis emoryi

Indian Tobacco
Nicotiana
trigonophylla

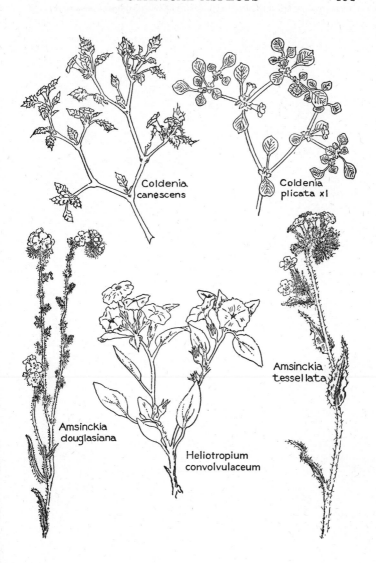

Coldenia
canescens

Coldenia
plicata x1

Amsinckia
douglasiana

Heliotropium
convolvulaceum

Amsinckia
tessellata

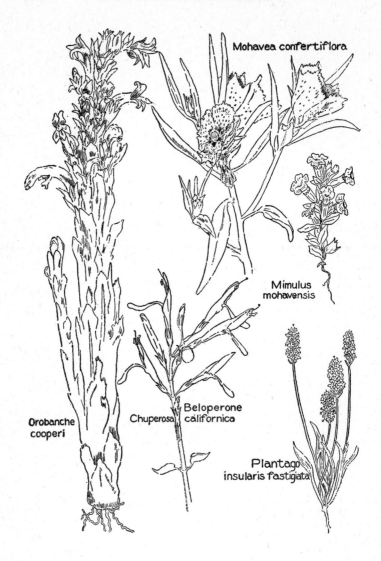

Mohavea confertiflora

Mimulus
mohavensis

Orobanche
cooperi

Chuperosa

Beloperone
californica

Plantago
insularis fastigiata

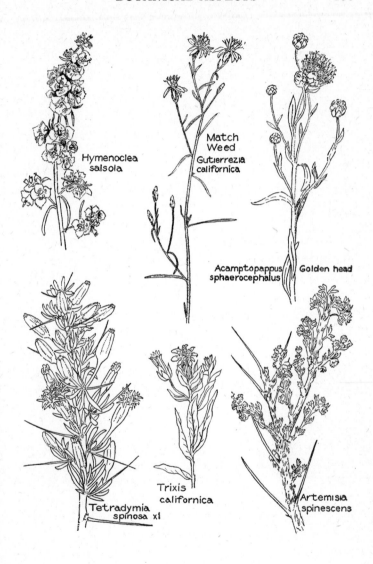

Hymenoclea
salsola

Match
Weed
Gutierrezia
californica

Acamptopappus   Golden head
sphaerocephalus

Tetradymia
spinosa x1

Trixis
californica

Artemisia
spinescens

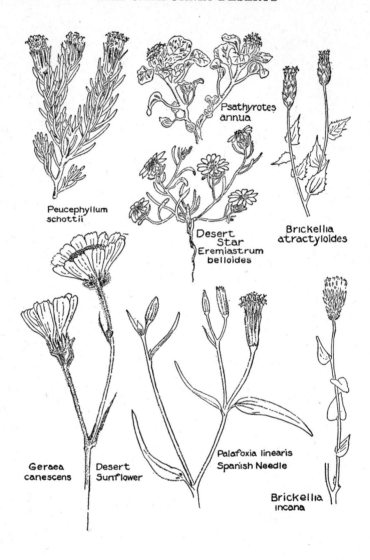

Peucephyllum
schottii

Psathyrotes
annua

Desert
Star
Eremiastrum
belloides

Brickellia
atractyloides

Geraea
canescens

Desert
Sunflower

Palafoxia linearis
Spanish Needle

Brickellia
incana

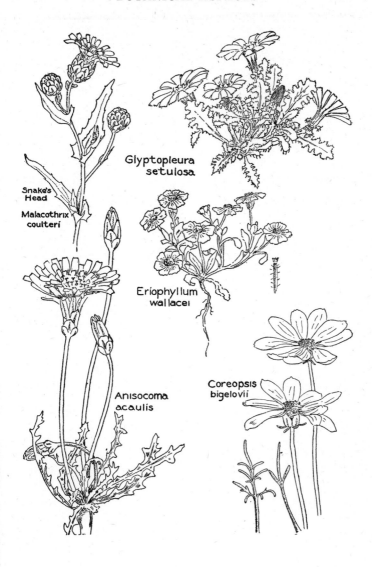

Glyptopleura
setulosa

Snake's
Head

Malacothrix
coulterí

Eriophyllum
wallacei

Anisocoma
acaulis

Coreopsis
bigelovii

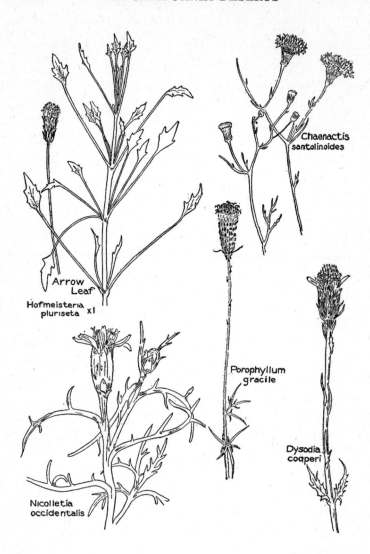

Chaenactis
santolinoides

Arrow
Leaf
Hofmeisteria
pluriseta x1

Porophyllum
gracile

Dysodia
cooperi

Nicolletia
occidentalis

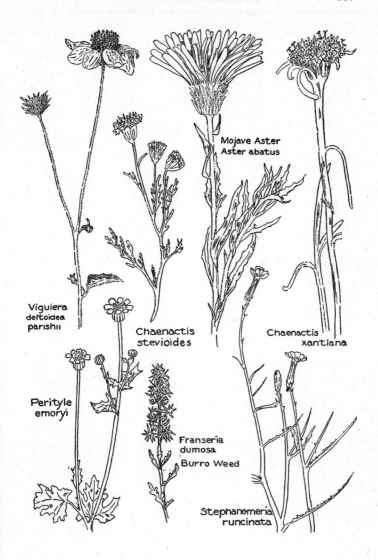

Mojave Aster
Aster abatus

Viguiera
deltoidea
parishii

Chaenactis
stevioides

Chaenactis
xantiana

Perityle
emoryi

Franseria
dumosa
Burro Weed

Stephanomeria
runcinata

CHAPTER XIII

FUNGI, FERNS, AND GRASSES

DESERTS with their great paucity of soil humus and scanty rainfall are seldom thought of as the home of fungi, but many specialized forms have adapted themselves to the severe conditions and from time to time show up in great abundance. When the rains dampen the soil they are able to perfect their growth in a remarkably short time. There are evidently more animal droppings and bits of decaying vegetation beneath the soil than one would suspect.

Shortly after rains and perhaps for some time afterward we see, springing up along roadsides and along the borders of the dry streamways, great numbers of that large, beautiful, glaring-white, puffball, *Podaxon farlowii.* The bulbous, club-shaped tops, covered with elongated, rectangular scales, often stand four or five inches above the ground. The scales gradually come off, leaving old specimens, which persist sometimes for months, smooth and brown. A very similar if not identical puffball is said to be found in the arid wastes of the Sahara and some of the other Old World deserts.

Gyrophragmium delelei, another conspicuous fungus, is much less common, but occasionally it pushes up in great numbers through the sands of washes. The rounded, leathery, spore-bearing sac or pileus, almost the size of one's fist, looks outwardly like a puffball but when examined is seen to have gills like a mushroom, and on these the spores are borne. Probably this is the same as a Mediterranean species of like appearance.

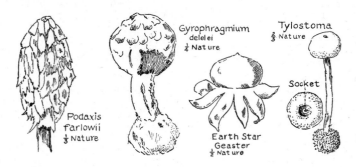

Gyrophragmium
delelei
¼ Nature

Tylostoma
⅔ Nature

Socket

Podaxis
farlowii
⅓ Nature

Earth Star
Geaster
½ Nature

The tylostomas are little, tall-stalked puffballs with a peculiar socket at the base of the peridium into which the long stipe is inserted. A small, button-like, basal disk or bulb, consisting of the mycelia and intermingled sand grains, generally comes up when the plant is pulled from the sand. *Tylostoma campestre* is the common species.

Some of the earth stars (*Geaster*) are always turning up in unexpected places. These little globular puffballs have coverings which are distinctly two-layered. The outer layer splits into spreading, star-shaped segments, while the inner layer remains intact except for a little chimney-like pore through which the black powdery spores come out.

Quite a number of rusts occur on plants of the desert area. These fungi depend for their existence entirely upon the living cells of the plants on which they are found as continuous parasites. Some of them have alternate hosts, living during one part of their existence on one species of plant and during another on another plant. Some alternate hosts are as different as the oak and a grass. Some of the common and interesting ones are mentioned in connection with their plant hosts. (See page 172.)

Many of the dull-hued rocks of arid regions are ornamented with the bright colors of encrusting lichens. An entirely new and engaging pleasure may be derived from a study and collection of the various forms.

The largest and finest splashes of vivid color occur on the north and northeast faces of black lava blocks of the Mohave region. Here, receiving the least exposure to the drying winds, the red, rock-wall lichen (*Caloplaca murorum*) paints the rock surface a striking reddish-brown, and *Acarospora chlorophana* spreads its coat of brilliant yellowish-green. With them may be growing *Lecanora saxicola,* another dainty, rock-hugging form of blue-gray hue.

Among the next most conspicuous lichens are *Acarospora epilutescens* (silver gray) and *Candelariella vitellina* (a deep, golden yellow), the last particularly beautiful when growing with other colorful species. Some of the black lichens occupy the sides of rocks in the most exposed situations, seeming to mind neither scorching sun nor desiccating winds.

Though in summer the withered plants apparently are as dry as the rock surfaces themselves, they are never without moisture. In winter they often get dampness directly from the rains which fall upon them, but in summer, says Dr. Albert Herre, "it is highly probable that the great diurnal drop in temperature which comes in all arid regions with the advent of darkness is likewise accompanied by a deposition of moisture or at least an increase in water content of desert lichens."

"When one considers," Dr. Herre further says, "that the temperature drops 30 to 35 degrees F. every night during summer months, it is apparent that without any increase in the actual amount of water present there is a great increase in the percentage of moisture, and it is believed by some of us that the lichens are able to take advantage of this relative increase and absorb enough moisture to maintain their vitality during the long, hot, dry season.

"That desert conditions are, in the main, unfavorable to the growth of lichens as a whole is shown by the limited number of genera and species represented, while a considerable number of those found are able to maintain themselves only in the most favorable spots, such as under overhanging rocks on the north side of cliffs within crevices. But that some species are perfectly at home in the midst of the most adverse desert conditions of excessive light and dryness is shown by the fact that almost everywhere the rocks are just as thickly covered with lichens as in other regions of greater humidity and less sunshine. The desert does not lack in number of individuals, but in number of species of lichens able to adapt themselves to its conditions."

It appears reasonable to believe that the presence of desert varnish is sometimes due to organic agencies such as the growth and disintegration of lichens. Dr. J. D. Loudermilk, who has examined many of the dark, "varnished" rock areas of the flat mesas of the Mohave Desert, noticed that they frequently occur as well-defined, circular patches in areas of similar but uncoated rocks. Investigation showed that the dark rock-surfaces were in many instances covered with colonies of small, almost microscopic, incrusting lichens. It is thought that the acids secreted by the lichens corrode the outer layers of the rocks and that the dissolved minerals, after having been taken up by the plants, are again deposited as oxides on the rock surfaces after the death of the lichens.

We are so accustomed to associate ferns with regions of dampness that it may be a surprise to many to know that at least twelve species belonging to three different genera are found in the territory under consideration. Subjected almost constantly to the drying winds, they have uniquely modified not only their structure but also their life histories in order to protect themselves from excessive transpiration and the caprices of an arid climate. The fronds are unusually small and thick and the pinnae multiplied and much divided. Some desert ferns have viscid coatings of wax, others are densely woolly or are clad in an armor of overlapping scales or hair which serves both as a protection and as a moisture-retaining covering.

These ferns must make their entire growth in the winter and spring season of rain and be ready to spend the dry summer days in dormancy. "But these rains," as the late S. B. Parish said, "are small in amount at any one time, they are uncertain, and the moisture is liable to be speedily evaporated by drying winds. Their fronds, therefore, unfold at once as soon as moistened by the first showers and resume life at the point where they dropped its functions, perhaps months ago. How long this active life may continue depends wholly upon the meteorological conditions. So long as moisture is attainable there is no cessation; but as soon as it fails, active life is suspended. In this condition the fern appears dead; the frond is dry and crumbles in the fingers;

the stipe and rhizome are brittle and break up in handling.
These resting fronds assume various forms. Many curl up
into more or less compact balls, exposing to the air the back
of the frond, which is the most heavily protected."

The golden-back fern (*Pityrogramma triangularis*) as
well as the coffee fern (*Pellaea andromadaefolia*) and the
bird's foot (*Pellaea mucronata*), so common in the southern
California foothills, reach the desert borders but are not
generally found far to the eastward. It is the cloak ferns of
the genus *Notholaena* and *Cheilanthes,* with their coverings
of woolly hairs, that are most successful in the more arid,
interior deserts. Four species of cloak ferns occur in the
shelter of rocks, Parry's cloak fern (*N. parryi*) being the
most widespread. This has pinnae so densely hairy that they
look like pellets of wool. Jones's cloak fern (*N. jonesii*),

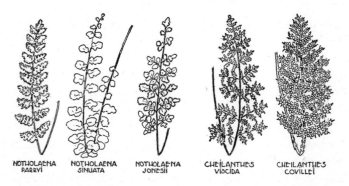

NOTHOLAENA PARRYI   NOTHOLAENA SINUATA   NOTHOLAENA JONESII   CHEILANTHES VISCIDA   CHEILANTHES COVILLEI

with its few scattered, leathery pinnae, is extensive in distribution but very rare. The sinuate cloak fern (*N. sinuata*)
is known in California only from the Providence Mountains.

The lip ferns, so called because of the in-rolling of the
edges of the sori, are represented by the viscid lip fern

(*Cheilanthes viscida*) with its remarkably sticky herbage (first collected by Dr. C. C. Parry and Mr. J. G. Lemmon, pioneer botanical explorers, at Whitewater), and *C. feei* of the Providence Mountains with dense, close hair on the under surface of the fronds. Coville's lip fern (*C. covillii*) is a fine little plant with closely set, beady end-segments, found plentifully not only in the desert mountains but also in some of the foothills nearer the coast.

Dry desert canyons would seem to hold little promise of our finding the delicate, water-loving maidenhair ferns, but in damp recesses of rocky grottoes or under shelving banks in the box canyons we sometimes come upon them; both are coastal species which have found footing in the deserts, or perhaps they are holdovers from a time when the deserts enjoyed a moister climate.

Vying with the ferns in meeting the conditions of almost perennial drought are the little-noticed, moss-like selaginellas. In the canyons and on the hillsides of the mountains near Palm Springs, and southward along the Colorado Desert's western border, the arid selaginella (*Selaginella eremophila*), with strong, flattened, bright-green branches which root beneath, is growing in large cushions at the foot of rocks, sometimes mingling with the ascending branches of the coastal selaginella (*S. bigelovii*). Differing in foliage characters from all other Pacific Coast species is *S. leucobryoides,* found in the Panamint and Providence mountains. The most striking of its characteristics are "the extremely short, pure white, but opaque, setae of the leaves and the condensed, rosette-like arrangement of the very short branches" (Maxon).

No fewer than thirty-three kinds of grasses are listed

from the California deserts. The dominant, conspicuous species are of the perennial bunch type. Galleta (pronounced locally Guy-ee-et'-ta) grass (*Hilaria rigida*), an erect grass about a foot high, is plentiful in many of the basins of both deserts. Its stiffish, felty-haired stems are rich in nourishment for grazing animals, and the cowmen always count it a stroke of good luck when they find it growing near enough to water holes and springs to make it available for feed. Inspection of the stem bases soon reveals large bulbous galls about an inch in diameter which appear like little fat ears of popcorn. These deformities, the interiors of which are hard as wood, are caused by a large eurytomid wasp (*Harmolita*), whose larvae develop within the tissues. A chance to see good stands of galleta grass is offered the traveler in West Cronese Valley on the road between Barstow and Las Vegas. In the high deserts of Inyo County and the Great Basin is another galleta grass (*Hilaria jamesii*) with smooth, hairless stems. Indian rice (*Oryzopsis hymenoides*) is frequent in porous soils, particularly on blown sand. The diffuse panicles bear hosts of large, plump seeds which are much relished by grazing animals. It is one of our most beautiful grasses and among our few sand-binding species. A very common and very handsome bunch grass of the high desert valleys is the desert needle grass (*Stipa speciosa*). It grows about a foot high and is plentiful among the junipers. Good open stands may be seen to advantage by the traveler between Cajon summit and Victorville. The blackened tufts of dead specimens are often very conspicuous.

After spring rains the little frost grass (*Triodia pulchella*) comes up in enormous quantities and, true to its common name, makes the desert where it grows appear as if covered with frost. The little clumps are often three or four inches across. The short, slender stems have a peculiar way of bending over and taking root again.

About the desert springs and along some of the tiny streams of the canyons occurs the common reed (*Phragmites communis*), with stems four or five feet high. In damp, alkaline soils, salt grass (*Distichlis spicata*) is often very abundant and is about the only plant that takes root there. It saved the life of many a hungry mule and ox in the days of pioneer travel.

CHAPTER XIV

SHRUBS

THE desert is surprisingly rich in the number of its woody
herbs and shrubs, the general coloration of which is
gray-green. To their dry, gray barks and hair-covered leaves
is due the monotonous aspect of much of the arid Southwest.
Only along or near moist streamways and washes or in the
semi-sheltered canyons of the higher mountains do the shrubs
attain sizable proportions. In the broad, practically waterless valleys, where arid conditions are intensified, most of
them grow no higher than a man's knee. The farther one
penetrates northeastward into the desert's interior the more
stunted the shrubs become. The number of species also
rapidly dwindles until we encounter, in some of the broad
basins of the eastern Mohave Desert, great areas whose only
conspicuous plants are those great water-conservers, the
creosote bush and the burro-weed. In parts of Panamint
Valley's parched floor even the burro-weed cannot withstand
the terrific struggle, and creosote alone braves the hot winds
and glaring light of a cruel summer sun. Because they are
well-spaced and equally exposed to light from all sides, the
characteristic form of most desert shrubs is globular or

167

hemispherical. All unsheltered desert perennials are subject to strong winds, and this results in a low, squat form which is a distinct advantage to them. The extensive root systems, built primarily for the absorption of moisture, serve as extraordinarily trusty anchors in times of stress.

The physical texture and chemical composition of the rocks of which mountains are built influences not only the type of flora but also the altitude to which the desert plants ascend the slopes. Mountains of granite and limestone favor the retention of moisture in the surface rocks much better than mountains of coarse-textured rhyolite and lavas. The Granite Mountains north of Amboy, the New York Mountains, the Old Woman Mountains, and Clark Mountain for this reason support a good mantle of brush far down their slopes, whereas other neighboring mountains of approximately the same altitude but made of volcanic rock are barren, even at their summits, of all but the hardiest desert shrubs.

In the upland belts of junipers and tree yuccas the predominant shrubs are the tetradymias, rabbit brushes, and senecios. Many of these come into flower late in the season, making the areas gay with shades of yellow. In the late spring, when the blue sage (*Salvia carnosa pilosa*) bursts into bloom, many of the high mesas of the Mohave are masses of brilliant sky blue.

Below the zone of tree yuccas, the creosote bush (*Larrea tridentata* var. *glutinosa*) takes possession. About the only place it does not grow is in the soils poisoned by sulphates or in the flat, salt-incrusted lake beds. Often it occurs in uncountable numbers and in almost pure stands, giving a lovely, brownish-green aspect to the floors of the spacious basins of the Mohave region. The seeds are slow to germinate and it takes peculiar combinations of heat and moisture to start the young plant. Except in spots, young bushes are certainly not plentiful. Most of the large shrubs appear to be very old. It is the lack of soil water which probably accounts for the amazingly regular spacing of the plants. Those round, brown or green balls, each about the size of a small walnut, which appear on the stems, are made by the creosote gall-midge (*Asphondylia auripila*). Though outwardly covered by hundreds of soft, dwarfed leaves, the interiors of the galls are hard and woody, and in this portion the larvae develop.

Associated with the creosote bush, especially in the higher elevations of the Mohave Desert, is the spiny hop sage (*Grayia spinosa*), the winged fruits of which are often tinged with rich shades of pink and maroon. There too are found the scraggly salazaria, with its bladder-like pods, and the very twiggy coleogyne. The last often occurs in such pure stands on the high alluvial fans that the whole area of dominance is colored a military blue-gray.

Species of ephedra or Mexican tea occur in similar situations. The ephedras have been given many common names: Mormon tea, teamster's tea, desert tea, Brigham tea, squaw tea, and canatello are just a few of the names in common use among the desert folk, who make a beverage of it by boiling a handful of the stems for a few minutes in water. All of the ephedras have long-jointed, fluted stems which bear minute, scale-like leaves at the nodes. The male plants are showy in spring and bear, in abundance, catkins with prominent, protruding yellow stamens of remarkable beauty. The California ephedra (*Ephedra californica*), with yellowish-green stems and leaf scales arranged in threes, is the commonest one. The spindle-shaped swellings on the stems are caused by a tiny, slender fly, the fusiform gall-fly (*Lasioptera ephedrae*), belonging to the same family of gall-makers (*Cecidomyiidae*) as the creosote gall-midge.

The shrubby paroselas call attention to themselves by their brilliant royal-purple, pea-like flowers. Most of them have herbage which is highly glandular and they give off, when crushed, an agreeable spicy odor. At least one species (*Parosela emoryi*) yielded a yellow dye to the Indians. The center of distribution of the paroselas is Mexico, where more than one hundred and twenty species are known.

The two species of krameria (*Krameria parvifolia* and *canescens*) are low, thorny shrubs, conspicuous in the vernal season because of their lovely wine-colored flowers and later because of their many odd, spine-tipped fruits. The kramerias derive most of their nourishment parasitically with the aid of peculiar root-pads which rest like saddles on the roots of other plants.

With gray-green stems, woefully naked for eleven months of the year, the desert cassias suddenly become in late April the showiest plants of the washes and mesas. Such a wealth of yellow flowers is seldom seen among desert shrubs. *Cassia armata* is the common species.

Franseria or white burro-weed (*Franseria dumosa*) is probably the second most abundant shrub of our southwestern deserts. It is a low, rounded bush of grayish hue generally found filling in gaps between the rather orderly-spaced creosote bushes. It is a most excellent browsing plant, four or five large bushes making a day's food for a burro. I cannot imagine why the animals like the bitter stuff.

Along the clayey banks of washes at low elevations one

is quite likely to see the goat-nut (*Simmondsia californica*), an erect, very drought-resistant shrub about three or four feet high, possessing ovoid, gray-green leaves, which are remarkably leathery and thick. It bears a nut which rodents evidently consider not at all bad eating, for in autumn we often run across stores of the nuts which have been gathered and hidden under rocks by mice and the little antelope chipmunks. Cattle, when driven by hunger, crop the leaves closely.

If among the creosote bushes you find a very spiny shrub on which are many little red or green, tomato-like fruits you may be certain you have found one of the lyciums or wolf bushes. The tubular flowers, colored white, pale purple, or lavender, are borne in abundance among the fascicles of small leathery or somewhat fleshy leaves. *Lycium pallidum,* of the Mohave Desert, with lavender to yellow, short, trumpet-shaped flowers, is the most decorative. The quail are fond of the juicy red fruits, which at times furnish their sole water supply.

Several shrubby herbaceous perennials are conspicuous in the sand washes of the Mohave Desert. Among them are the fine - stemmed match weeds (*Gutierrezia*), which we prize above all other plants as tinder for our fires, the gritty-leaved sand-paper bush (*Petalonyx thurberi*), and several of the resin-filled ericamerias. The ashy-green *Ericameria paniculata* is particularly a prominent wash plant of the northern Mohave Desert. It is associated with senecio (*S. douglasii*) and scale-broom (*Lepidospartum squamatum*), and after the summer rains they all burst into yellow bloom, attracting great numbers of insects. The refreshing bright-green herbage of the foul-odored hymenoclea (*Hymenoclea salsola*) completes the pleasing picture. Its strong roots penetrate deep to the moist wash-sands and it manages to stay green during most of the year. A smut fungus (*Puccinia splendens*) often causes the stems to break open and turn black.

Along dry streamways of the Colorado Desert there are several shrubs particularly common. One of these is the bladder-pod (*Isomeris arborea*). It blooms throughout the year and its yellow blossoms often lend the only bits of bright color to the otherwise drab scene. Though the foliage is foul-scented, we admire the plant for the delicate appearance of its flowers and its pendant, inflated fruits. The desert lavender (*Hyptis emoryi*), another large, wash-inhabiting shrub with wand-like branches, compels our notice by means of its almost constant show of woolly, blue-gray masses of minute, mint-like flowers. The plant is not tolerant of heavy frosts and is for this reason largely confined to the southern desert. It is a great bee-plant and often the special nesting site of the plumbeous gnatcatcher and the verdin. The peculiar, blackish growths on the woody parts of the stems are due to a rust fungus (*Puccinia distorta*). The presence of the smut is one of the chief causes of the large number of dead limbs. In the same dry streamways grows the scarlet-flowered beloperone (*Beloperone californica*), one of the earliest and most persistent bloomers of the year. Because of the color and form of its flowers, many mistake it for a bush pentstemon. Its tubular flowers are often visited by humming birds for the nectar, hence its Spanish name, "chuparosa," meaning "sucking rose." The house finches sometimes bite off the corolla tubes to get at the nectar glands and ovaries.

When we approach the dry-lake bottoms we encounter a whole new assemblage of plants—plants which must draw upon the highly alkaline soils for their moisture. Among these are cattle spinach (*Atriplex polycarpa*), sarcobatus, suaeda, the ink weed (*Allenrolfea occidentalis,* named after Allen Rolfe, one-time botanist at Kew Gardens, London), and several kinds of isocoma.

Saltbushes are plants inhabiting alkaline soils throughout all of the Western deserts. They are often tolerant of very dry soils. The most widespread Mohavean saltbush is *Atriplex confertifolia,* known as sheep-fat or spiny saltbush. The low, compact bushes are not wholly confined to alkaline areas but are generally distributed among shrubs of the broad basins of the Mohave region from the vicinity of Barstow northward. In the Salton Sink, *A. canescens* is very abundant both in dry and damp soils, and *A. lentiformis,* the quail bush, forms enormous thickets in the damp, saline soils and rich bottom-lands of the Salton Sink and the Colorado River. These shrubby plants offer to the quail, to roadrunners, desert sparrows, and other birds very adequate protection from birds of prey. The handsome, silver-leaved desert holly is one of the salt bushes which flourishes best in the hot, gravelly hills of the Mohave Desert, but it is not at all uncommon on the Colorado Desert among the low hills to the east of the Salton Sea.

In those barren hills and low mountains which lie about the bases of the Santa Rosa and Laguna mountains of the Colorado Desert, in soil so rocky, dry, and alkaline that the hardiest desert shrubs grow scarcely above three spans high, colonies of the desert agave (*Agave deserti*) flourish and multiply. The whole aspect of the plant, from the rosette of thick, blue-green, spine-armed leaves to the tall, rigid scapes bearing the leathery flowers, well matches the arid environment.

On the same day that Emory and his forlorn soldiers saw their first Washingtonia palms (page 189), they came upon this agave and through thickets of it they rode for miles. "The sharp thorns terminating every leaf of this plant," said Emory, "were a great annoyance to our dismounted and weary men whose legs were now almost bare. A number of these plants were cut by the soldiers, and the body of them used as food. The day was intensely hot and the sand deep; the animals, inflated with water and rushes, gave way by scores: and, although we advanced only 16 miles, many did not arrive at camp until 10 o'clock that night. It was a feast day for the wolves which followed in packs close to our track, seizing our deserted brutes and making the air resound with their howls as they battled for the carcasses."

Of the shrubby yuccas, the Mohave yucca (*Yucca mohavensis*) is the most widespread. Its stems, armed with long, yellow-green, dagger-like leaves, sometimes reach upward higher than a man's head. Within the far eastern borders of California grows *Yucca baccata,* a plant easily distinguished from our other desert yuccas by its grayish blue-green leaves and enormous fruits. Its leaves are all basal. On the high slopes of the New York Mountains and vicinity it consorts with junipers, Mohave yuccas, tree yuccas, and piñons.

About once a year I receive from some desert prospector a shrub made up wholly of rigid, gray-green, sharp-pointed stems, and with the gift comes the remark, "This is the thorn out of which they made the crown for Christ when he was crucified." Of course it is not, but the situation is hard to explain to the prospector. Specimens are generally collected near Hayfields, about twenty-five miles east of Mecca, where the spiny shrub grows in considerable abundance. *Holocanthus emoryi,* as it is known to botanists, is a near relative of the Chinese tree of heaven (*Ailanthus*). It is common enough in southern Arizona but seems to have established itself in only a few places on the deserts here. The dense clusters of nut-like fruits make good donkey feed, but the plants are otherwise worthless to man.

One of the thorniest and most striking plants of the desert area is the ocotillo (*Fouquieria splendens*), which, because of its many vicious spines, is often erroneously brigaded with the cacti. Ascending from a stout basal stem, the many long, cane-like, thorn-armed branches reach upward, sometimes to a height of twenty feet. The time of flowering is late April, but rains at unusual times cause the plants to come into full leaf and to blossom out of season. The panicles of scarlet, tubular flowers atop the graceful stems make the desert hills and *bajadas* aflame with color. Plants bearing a hundred or more ascending branches, each bearing its brilliant flowers, are not at all uncommon.

The true sagebrush (*Artemisia tridentata*), bearing spatula-shaped leaves of gray-green color, occupies only a few high-altitude areas where the rainfall is fairly well distributed throughout the year. Though it is familiar enough to residents of Utah and Nevada, it is not well known among desert people in California. To many campers the sweet-scented smoke floating upward from sagebrush campfires is rivaled as a provoker of pleasant memories only by the aromatic smoke of burning creosote twigs.

The cacti belong almost entirely to the New World. They are widely distributed over the arid Southwest but are abundant only in those places where water supplies are seasonally plentiful. Such conditions obtain in the higher desert ranges and on many of the encircling alluvial fans whose washes carry the rapid run-off of summer cloudbursts and winter rains. Loose gravels or sandy, well-drained soils seem absolutely necessary for prolific growth. The long corky-barked roots, many of them several yards long, are purposely laid close to the soil-surface and are always eager to take up the water of either shallow or penetrating rains. Of very greatest interest is the fact that the cacti are our only desert plants storing water in the stems. This stored water is given up very reluctantly even during the hottest days. But the ingress of carbon dioxide, which, with water, is the chief raw material utilized by the plant in the manufacture of its food, is also checked at the same time, and this is the reason why cacti are generally such slow growers.

The cactus family is here represented by at least ten species of Opuntia, three species of the genus Cereus, four of Echinocactus, and possibly four of Mamillaria. Of these, two are wholly Colorado Desert forms, nine entirely Mohavean; the remaining ten are common to both deserts.[1]

The opuntias or prickly-pear cacti are divided into two groups—those with cylindrical stems (*Cylindropuntia*), and those with flattened stems (*Platyopuntia*).

Opuntia with cylindrical stems.—Darning-needle cactus (*Opuntia ramosissima*), as its specific name implies, is a much-branched, erect shrub with slender, very woody stems.

---

[1] When the deserts are more thoroughly explored and the cacti are more carefully studied the list will doubtless be extended.

Each of the joints is about two inches long and bears long spines (1½ inches) covered with yellow sheaths. The joints during summer frequently turn reddish. It is found on both deserts eastward to Nevada and Arizona. The flowers are purplish but not showy.

Bigelow's cholla (*O. bigelovii*), sometimes called "bad cholla," is the spiniest and most vicious of all our cacti. Individual plants often congregate to form thickets on the dissected benches and alluvial fans issuing from the mouths of the large canyons. No other species presents such interesting forms nor gives such fine color effects. The tracts of chollas with their blendings of greens and browns are always alluring. Because the seeds are usually sterile, propagation is effected principally by detachment of the fleshy joints. The thickly interwoven needles are strongly barbed and once in the flesh stick with persistence and leave a painful wound. This species is seldom found on the Mohave Desert but is plentiful on the Colorado Desert.

Beaver Tail Cactus

Bigelow's Cholla

Mohave Niggerhead

Deerhorn Cactus

Deer-horn cactus (*O. echinocarpa*) is surely our commonest species. The compact crowns are widespreading and made of interwoven, loosely branched joints, three to six inches long and one inch or more thick. The spines, both long and short ones, are yellowish and covered with papery sheaths which when chewed taste like witch-hazel. The flowers are yellow, sometimes tinged with red, and are not particularly pleasing. This cactus is common on both deserts eastward to Utah and Arizona. It seldom forms thickets. The handsomest specimens I have ever seen grow on the sands to the northeast of the symmetrical cinder cone directly north of Little Lake.

The spiny-fruited cholla (*O. acanthocarpa*) is an erect species somewhat resembling deer-horn cactus but of more open growth. From the few stout main stems project numerous green branches, the joints of which bear elongate tubercles armed with groups of yellow spines, each about an inch long. The flowers are yellow to reddish. This cactus is plentiful in the higher mountains of the eastern Mohave Desert.

The club-jointed opuntia (*O. parishii*) is a rarely noticed cactus, even though it possesses such handsome ovate fruits. The flattened, gray-brown spines adorn the short, prostrate, club-like stems in radiating clusters. The roots are on the under side of the joints. The spreading mats, made of joints well-hidden with spines, have all the appearance of being dried up and dead. This is principally a Mohavean species found at high altitudes (4,000 to 5,000 feet). Its blossoms are said to last but an hour.

Opuntias with flat stems. — Beaver-tail or slipper-sole cactus (*O. basilaris*) is a low, spreading species having joints without spines but viciously armed with myriads of brown, prickly hairs called glochids. It is widely distributed from sea-level to 8,000 feet, varying much in form and in the

luxuriance of its joints, according to altitude. Its brilliant
rose-purple flowers appear most handsome against the neu-
tral gray background of flat stems. The Cahuilla Indians,
after removing the hairs by rolling the parts in the sand,
cook the tender fruits and succulent stems with meat and
pronounce it to be an excellent dish.

Grizzly bear cactus (*O. ursina*) is a fine species with
ascending joints almost completely hidden by the remarkable,
long, ashy-gray or white spines (3 to 10 inches long) which
bend under touch like bristles. It has been much sought by
cactus fanciers, and the beds which are locally abundant on
the Mohave Desert have been repeatedly raided.

Hedgehog cactus (*O. erinacea*) is somewhat similar to
woolly-bear cactus in general appearance, but it has shorter
joints and the brownish spines are less flexible. It is locally
abundant on high gravelly or stony slopes of the Mohave
Desert and eastward to Nevada, Utah, and Arizona.

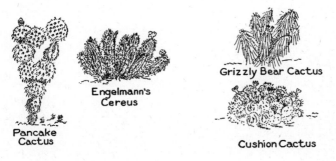

Pancake
Cactus

Engelmann's
Cereus

Grizzly Bear Cactus

Cushion Cactus

The remarkable pancake cactus (*O. chlorotica*) has great,
flat, orbicular joints "like pancakes" (3 to 8 inches in diameter), light green in color, and armed with many close-set
groups of handsome, golden - yellow spines. The trunk is

almost as spiny as the joints. This large, erect, stout-stemmed cactus is usually found singly in rocky situations on the slopes of the desert mountains.

The Mohave opuntia (*O. mojavensis*) is a prostrate species of the *bajadas* and mountains of the Mohave Desert. It has large, flat, round joints (8 to 12 inches in diameter) resembling those of *O. chlorotica*. On the upper border of the joints are numerous clusters of golden spines. The stout, rigid needles, from one to one-and-a-half inches long and borne in clusters of two to six, are white but with reddish-brown bases. The flowers are yellow, the fruits spineless.

All of our cacti of the genus *Cereus* and *Echinocactus* possess globate or columnar stems bearing ridges on which the spines occur in bundles. In the genus *Cereus* the spines are borne below the summit of the ribs; in the genus *Echinocactus,* at the summit. The flowers are often brilliantly colored.

Engelmann's cereus (*C. engelmanni*), a handsome, purple-flowered species, is a rival in beauty of the regal *Opuntia basilaris*. It is common in the rocky hills and wastes throughout our Southwestern deserts up to 8,000 feet altitude. The rounded stems, each about a foot long, diverge from a central point and are armed with brownish, radiating spines.

The Mohave cereus or cushion cactus (*C. mojavensis*) has long-spined stems about the size of baseballs, and these multiply until they form large cushions consisting of hundreds of stems; as many as six hundred stems have been counted in a cluster. The flowers are a brilliant deep red. It is a species occupying rocky situations.

Of the echinocacti the huge barrel cactus (*Echinocactus acanthodes*) is most spectacular and best known. The great, stout stems, sometimes five or six but more often two or three feet high, are armed with strong, rigid spines which vary in color from bright red to yellow. This species reaches its best development on the gravelly fans of alluvium of the Colorado Desert. It grows in sheltered situations in the mountains of the Mohave Desert up to altitudes of 3,500 feet. Trade rats often completely hollow out the stems in their search for green food and water and leave only a "basket" of needles.

Closely allied to this is the Mohavean niggerhead (*Echinocactus polycephalus*), which forms compact, rounded clumps of elongate, ovoid heads, each eight or ten inches in diameter. The general color of the heads as seen from a short distance is purplish. The flowers, arranged in a crowning circle, are yellow, and the dry fruits are very woolly with white matted hairs. It prefers to grow among rocks.

Much less frequently seen are the two other species, *E. polyancistrus* and *E. johnsonii*. Both are plants of the upper Mohave Desert and the dry mountains northward. They have simple stems and the spines are without rings. The elongate stems (8 to 12 inches high) of *E. polyancistrus* are covered with many straight and also many hooked spines, the latter brownish. Johnson's cactus, sometimes called beehive cactus, has short, cylindrical stems, four to nine inches high, bearing many awl-shaped spines which are enlarged at the base.

The mamillaria or nipple cacti are so named because of the many teat-like tubercles on which the spines are borne. Of the five species known to the state of California, four occur on the deserts. They are divided into two groups— those with central spines hooked, and those with all the spines straight. Of those with hooked spines, *Mamillaria tetrancistra* is probably best known. It occurs on both deserts. Graham's fish-hook cactus (*M. microcarpa*), having a white flower with a purple midvein, is confined wholly to the southern Colorado Desert. The straight-spined nipple cactus, *Mamillaria deserti,* grows in the mountains of the eastern Mohave Desert. The young plants are generally found half concealed in the gravel, but the neat attire of white, brown-tipped, interlocking spines makes them easy to find. The flowers, straw-colored or light lilac, open in late June. Alverson's mamillaria (*M. alversoni*), with light-purple flowers and with a dozen or more central, purple- or black-tipped spines to each nipple, is confined to the mountains to the north and east of the Salton Sea.

CHAPTER XV

TREES

WHERE the conditions of aridity are intense, such as over
the greater portion of the Mohave Desert and on rocky
mesas and hillsides of the Colorado Desert, trees are generally absent, but where the ground-water supply is fairly
abundant or plentiful, as in the large washes, along water
courses, and about the margins of the Salton Sea, trees of
low, spreading form flourish and often attain considerable
dimensions. By observing these trees for size and luxuriance,
it is possible to estimate with considerable accuracy the
abundance and depth of underground waters.

One of the best of ground-water indicators is the honey,
or straight-podded, mesquite (*Prosopis chilensis*), a desert
tree of high water requirements found typically in thick forests in the alluvial soils of flood plains and lake basins. You
will find a few of the trees about almost every fresh-water
spring, no matter how isolated. Where the mesquite occurs in
the dry beds of water-courses it has served as one of the sur-
est means of successfully locating places to dig wells. One of
the worst insect enemies of this tree is the mesquite girdler
(*Oncideres pustulatus*), a small, gray, long-haired beetle,

with rust-colored spots on its back. The larvae burrow beneath the bark and the adults girdle the small stems. In either case the woody parts are eventually killed. The larvae of the round-headed mesquite borer (*Megacyllene antennatus*) work in the dry wood. These are white, robust grubs fully 1½ inches long, which quickly reduce the soundest cordwood to powder. Human woodcutters, in order to protect their wood, burn the bark and destroy the eggs.

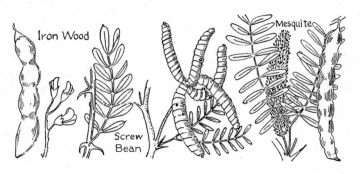

Closely allied to the honey, or straight-podded, mesquite, is the screw-bean (*Prosopis pubescens*), a small-stemmed tree first collected by Dr. Thomas Coulter on the old San Felipe Trail. It grows abundantly along the Colorado River, also along the water course of the Mohave River between Oro Grande and Daggett and again in Cave Canyon. Here the soil is deep and water is plentiful. In the Salton Sink it is common in almost pure stands near the north end of the Salton Sea. We encounter a few trees in sheltered canyon bottoms as far north as Death Valley. Trees in favored localities are known to grow to a height of 25 feet. The small holes often found in the curiously twisted seed-pods of the screw-bean probably mark the exits of a small desert weevil

(*Bruchus desertorum*) which breeds in the seeds of this and the honey mesquite. An Indian told me that these insect-infested pods were never discarded when the beans were ground up by the squaws to make the amole, or porridge.

The cat's-claw (*Acacia greggii*), most appropriately called "tear-blanket" by John W. Audubon and "wait-a-minute" by some of the other early travelers, is our only native acacia and like the acacias of the African deserts drops its leaves in the winter season (the Australian desert acacias are evergreen). In the windswept San Gorgonio Pass near Banning it occurs as a low, dense, spreading shrub scarcely more than 1¼ feet high and shows most markedly the effects of exposure in modifying the form of plants. In the shelter of cliffs and in deep rock crevices it is a several-stemmed shrub, its slender, wand-like branches reaching a length of 6 or 7 feet. Its general habit is, however, more upright and it may become a tree fully 15 feet high. Its spiny branches afford a refuge for numerous small birds, the verdin being particularly partial to it when building its flask-shaped nest. The cat's-claw occurs in rocky washes and in gullies of the desert hillsides up to an altitude of 4,500 feet. The Providence Mountains mark its northern limit of occurrence. The wood is very hard and remarkably beautiful when finished.

Parasitic on both the mesquite and the cat's-claw is a pendulous, slender-branched mistletoe (*Phoradendron californicum*). It bears plentiful supplies of waxy-red berries. This is the mistletoe responsible for the ill-health and final death of so many of the ironwood trees (see page 186).

Other tree members of the pea family are the two green-barked palo verdes (*Cercidium microphyllum* and *Cercidium floridum*). Both occur as small shrubs to large trees in the detrital soil of the Colorado Desert washes and river bottoms, the first being generally distributed but the latter confined to the vicinity of the Colorado River. The leaves appear in March but soon drop, leaving the showy, pale-yellow flowers and the smooth, vividly green bark as the trees' only adornment. In deep, sandy washes of the Chuckawalla district I

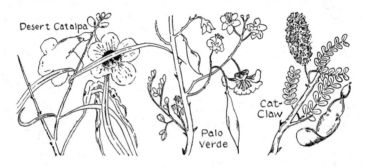

have seen trees with crowns 40 feet across. The palo verde is very intolerant of frost, and this accounts for its absence from most of the Mohave Desert.

The legumes are further represented by the spiny, much-branched, broad-crowned ironwood (*Olneya tesota*), which flourishes in most of the large sand-washes and on the stream-dissected alluvial fans of the Colorado Desert from Indio southward into Sonora and Lower California and eastward into Arizona. In its form, it is extremely variable; particularly is this true of the older trees whose sturdy, blackish trunks seem bent at every conceivable angle. Owing to the injuries caused by mistletoe, the trunks and branches frequently show great, rounded swellings a foot or more in diameter. The fragrant lavender or purple flowers appear in May and June, and by August the flat seed-pods are fat with the little brown seeds which in former years were so much prized by the Indians. Roasted, the seeds are said to have a rich, peanut-like flavor. When the young leaves first appear they are greatly relished by browsing animals, and in those happy days when we traveled about with donkeys I often tied the animals at night to a low, spreading tree, knowing for a certainty that their appetites would be well appeased by morning.

Although the dead ironwood is remarkably hard, the jaws of boring beetle larvae often reduce it to powder in a few months. The larvae prefer, however, to work in the smaller branches. The wood of the dead trees makes the finest and most lasting of all campfires and often when away from the desert I long for the delicious odor of the smoke which is connected with so many pleasant memories of engaging experiences of bygone nights.

The smoke tree (*Parosela spinosa*), like the palo verde, enjoys strong summer suns and is intolerant of heavy frosts. Its northern limit of growth is found about ten miles north of the Union Pacific Railway near Baker, California. The seeds germinate very readily after summer rains and the sandy washes are populated with numerous tiny seedling trees which all too often die because of the ephemeral supplies of moisture. When moisture is permanent the trees grow to a height of 10 or 15 feet. In their dress of silver-green thorns and abundant fragrant ornamental bloom they are one of the show sights of the desert. The flowering season is usually mid-June. In spring its spiny, leafless branches afford nesting-sites for verdins, gnatcatchers, and thrashers. A moonlight night spent in a smoke-tree forest is an experience never to be forgotten.

In the late spring and summer days the desert catalpa or so-called desert willow (*Chilopsis linearis*) cheers the wayfarer with its pendant green leaves and its wealth of gay, pink, tubular flowers. It is largely confined to the edges and beds of washes where in the deep, well-drained sands some moisture lingers to dampen the long and often deep roots. The desert willow is the food plant of that remarkable moth, *Eucaterva variaria,* whose white wings on the upper side appear as if sprinkled with fine flakes of mica (see illustration, page 61). The larvae build tough, gauzy, buff-colored cases in which they pupate. The old cocoons, each about an inch long, are found still clinging to the small stems in spring.

The athel or flowering tamarisk (*Tamarix gallica*) has escaped from its original plantings on ranches and now occurs about many of the alkaline springs of Death Valley and the Salton Basin. The minute seeds, terminated by plumes of hairs, are probably distributed by both winds and birds.

In mountains high enough to support a growth of piñons, the desert scrub oak (*Quercus dumosa* var. *turbinella*) with its tiny gray leaves is found. In some of the high valleys of the Little San Bernardino Mountains it forms a tree of generous proportions.

Rarest of all our arid-mountain trees is the hackberry (*Celtis douglasii*), known on the deserts of California only from a few localities in far eastern San Bernardino County. I have found it on Clark Mountain and in the New York Mountains.

One occasionally meets a few specimens of the Arizona ash (*Fraxinus velutina*) or its leather-leaved variety, *coriacea,* along the desert streams and about springs. It is a Great Basin tree common in southern Utah and southern Nevada.

The dwarf ash (*F. anomala*) is a species so un-ash-like that it is always a puzzler to the novice in tree lore. The leaves, instead of being compound, are usually simple and roundish, from 1½ to 2 inches across. It is truly a desert species and may be found, as a shrub or small tree, along washes of Clark Mountain and in the Providence and the Panamint ranges.

The Washingtonia palm (*Washingtonia filifera*) is a native tree of the Salton Basin and its bordering mountains. The extensive groves found north of Indio along the line of the San Andreas fault have been repeatedly burned by vandals until their former beauty is gone. Many small groups, still untouched and fortunately undiscovered by the public, lie hidden about water seeps in many of the little canyons in the Santa Rosa Range. The palm is an unfailing sign of the presence of water, but the quality is not necessarily good, since the trees are very tolerant of alkali. The first printed record of the finding of the Washingtonia palm is in *Emory's Reconnaissance* (1848). The party of weary travelers crossing the Colorado Desert had passed its western portals and after having journeyed a few miles beyond a spring called Ojo Grande, they met palms. "Here," says Emory, "on November 29, several scattered objects were seen projected against the cliffs and hailed by the Florida campaigners, some of whom were along, as old friends. They were the cabbage trees and marked the locale of a spring and a small patch of grass." This place at the head of Carrizo Creek Canyon is now known as Palm Springs. Then, as now, the moist plot about the palms was probably sodded with salt grass (*Distichlis spicata*), wire rush (*Juncus balticus*), and a sedge (*Scirpus americana*) known as "three-square" because of its triangular stems.

Dried and drying palms are generally found to be infested by the larvae of a robust bostrychid beetle (*Dinapate wrightii*), the California palm borer. The large galleries where the larvae fed and later pupated are regular features of old, weathered palm logs.

In the rocky hills bordering the Colorado River, from the Riverside Mountains southward toward Yuma, a few specimens of the giant sahuaros (*Cereus gigantea*) grow. They are California's largest cacti, and it is hoped the few specimens will long be preserved. The little elf owl, so common in southern Arizona, finding suitable environment here, lives in many of the deserted woodpecker holes found in the robust stems.

The tree yucca (*Yucca brevifolia*) is at once the most spectacular and the most characteristic tree of the Mohave Desert. In its various forms it occurs north through the high mountainous areas of the Death Valley region and eastward into Nevada, Utah, and Arizona; its southernmost station in California is, I believe, in the Iron Mountains of eastern Riverside County, where a few trees grow along the Aqueduct road between Boulder Well and Rice. As was the case with the Washingtonia palm, this yucca was given the name of cabbage tree by the pioneer travelers, and today it is often erroneously brigaded with the palms under the name of "yucca palm." The biology of this bizarre tree is still very imperfectly known and I have spent some very interesting hours studying the root system, noting the rapidity of its growth, and collecting the insects which congregate about the fruits and flowers, or bore, as larvae, in its sturdy branches. The two chief causes of branching of the tree yucca appear to be the dying of the terminal buds after flowering and the injury caused by the yucca-boring weevil (*Scyphophorus yuccae*). The larvae of this beetle, when ready for pupation, build in the ends of the branches peculiar, tough cases of frass, as the chewed-up, fibrous refuse from boring insects is called. The so-called petrified wood, so much prized as fuel by desert settlers, is made by the plant as it lays down silica in the cell walls in its attempt to wall off the injuries done by the borers, by fire, or by wind.

This tree propagates itself by means of seed and by sending out long, underground runners. We are especially interested in the young plants which spring from the runners, for it is upon these that the Navaho yucca borer (a butterfly, *Megathymus yuccae navaho*) lays her large eggs. When these hatch, the energetic larvae bore into the young plants and make their way to the large underground stems, where they feed and later pupate. Now the female butterfly seems to know that if she lays her eggs on the small-rooted, small-stemmed plants which spring from seeds there will be no food there for her larvae. In some uncanny way she is able to distinguish between the seedling plants and the runner plants —a distinction which man cannot readily make! Because the plants of runner origin alone are suited to her needs, the female, so far as is known, never lays her eggs upon the seedling plants.

The scrub juniper (*J. californica*) of the western Mohave and Colorado deserts, the Utah juniper (*J. californica utahensis*) of the eastern desert ranges, and the single-leaf piñon (*Pinus monophylla*) are among the most drought-resistant of our cone-bearing trees. They occur on most of the higher desert ranges that reach an elevation of 5,000 feet or over, often forming a fairly dense cover, particularly in deep, granitic soils. In the New York Mountains of eastern San Bernardino County, they associate with the two-needle nut-pine (*Pinus edulis*). Since the nuts of piñon trees are eagerly sought as food by rodents, human nut-hunters must be early in the field to get their share. The usual pine-nut harvest season is the middle of September. The commonest mistletoe of the scrub junipers is *Phoradendron densum,* the compact clumps of which adorn almost every tree.

The water-loving willows and cottonwoods thrust their roots into the moist soils of streamways and mark the location of a great number of the isolated springs found in canyon bottoms or on rocky hillsides. The cottonwoods (*Populus fremonti*) along the Mohave River intermittently mark the stream's long course through the desert as far east as Cave Canyon. In the branches of this cheerful tree hang long festoons of a mistletoe with yellowish-green leaves (*Phoradendron flavescens* var. *macrophyllum*). A peculiar, long-leaved variety of this cottonwood (*P. fremonti* var. *arizonica*) is found on the desert's edge at Snow Creek in the San Jacinto Mountains. The tall, handsome, slender-branched cottonwood of the Colorado delta, now so commonly planted along city streets and about ranches in the Imperial and Coachella valleys, is the MacDougall cottonwood (*P. fremonti* var. *MacDougallii*). It was introduced into the Salton Sink by the Southern Pacific Railway. Trees brought from Yuma were planted about the stations.

Forestiera (*F. neo-mexicana*) is a small tree belonging to the same great natural group as the olive. The bark is smooth, the leaves are simple, and the branches are opposite. This tree has a tendency to be gregarious, and small groups of them occur here and there in the high desert canyons.

CHAPTER XVI

TRAVEL HINTS

WRITERS, thinking only of the advertising value of their word pictures, have generally described the desert as a region of desolation, cheerless and dreary, a land of relentless heat, with every plant vested in thorns and every animal poisonous or savage. They have dwelt upon the difficulties and perils of travel in mule-and-wagon days and would have us think that it is equally difficult today to make our way by auto over the miles of desert roads. As a matter of fact, the desert is on the whole a friendly land, its beasts no fiercer than those found elsewhere; nor is travel in it, except in rare instances, unusually dangerous for those who use discretion in taking care of themselves and their motor cars. Several of the main highways are paved, and many of the minor "roads which lead to nowhere" are easily negotiated by the circumspect traveler.

Hazlitt reminds us that "there is nothing so pleasing as going on a journey." This is particularly true when the journey takes one to the unspoiled, untilled desert. There one is free of all ties, and if he is fortunate enough to have in any measure the spirit of the artist, the naturalist, or the mystic, his days of travel will be filled with wonder. The desert landscape is monotonous only to the uninformed.

Autumn and winter days are best for visits to the low-lying Colorado Desert. The winter nights may be nippy with cold, but the balmy, sunny days make one wish he might live perpetually in this out-of-door land of paradise. March marks the onset of the flower season, and then the whole country may be aglow with color and the air heavy with the sweet perfume of verbenas, primroses, and encelias. When in the warmth of April days the annuals of the Salton Basin begin to wilt and turn brown, the Mohavean blossoms are at their best. They continue blooming until late in May.

Halcyon days cannot be expected to last forever. All too frequently the times of quiet weather are interrupted by days of wind. The desert traveler must either learn to enjoy from time to time the wind's weird music and wild ways or leave the desert when the blustery days of the flower season arrive.

Even summer offers attractions to those who appreciate calm evenings, cloudless night skies, and fine, clear mornings. I prefer to avoid the heat of midday, but often in July and August I slip over the mountain passes to spend the night on the desert's edge. If the motor car is equipped for sleeping, or if one has a high cot, he need not fear that snakes or other creeping things will share the blankets with him. I must draw attention, though, to the danger of walking abroad on warm nights without a lantern or a flashlight, for it is certain that snakes are active then.

Really to appreciate the desert you must live close to its heart, walk upon its unbroken soil, and camp upon its clean sands. In choosing a campsite, the first thought should be given to finding shelter from possible wind and a level open place for the fire and the bed. I usually take to the sandy washes, where large smoke trees, palo verdes, and mesquites furnish wood and noonday shade. I often find delightful sheltered spots in the lee of great rocks or along the walls of canyons. In winter days the pockets along the edge of lava flows offer covert. Having five gallons of water with me, I am free to camp wherever I please.

Illustrative of day or week-end trips on which little more than a sight-seeing program is undertaken is the tour from Los Angeles to Palm Springs on the Colorado Desert, or to Red Rock Canyon, or to Barstow on the Mohave Desert. If several days are at one's disposal, real holiday journeys to Death Valley (7 days), to Lone Pine and Darwin (3 days), to El Centro and Yuma (4 days), to Needles (4 days), to Las Vegas, Nevada (5 days), are in order. The journey to Death Valley[1] is particularly delightful since it furnishes such a rich variety of scenic beauty. From November until May the trip may be made in comfort. To see the country to best

---

[1] Death Valley was constituted a National Monument by Presidential proclamation in February 1933. It comprises an area of 3,103 square miles, or 2,000,000 acres, and has as its peculiar interests a unique flora and marvelously interesting and beautiful geological formations. According to Dr. L. F. Noble it contains "rocks of all the great geological time divisions—Archean, Paleozoic, Mesozoic, Tertiary and Quaternary—whose aggregate thickness certainly exceeds 30,000 feet for the stratified rocks alone. Earth movements in the area have been so profound and so recurrent that the rock masses form a complex mosaic of crustal blocks isolated one from another by folding, faulting, tilting, igneous intrusion, erosion and buried under Quaternary alluvium." It is truly a geologists' paradise. The serious student will do well to read Dr. Nobles' paper, "Rock Formations of Death Valley, California," *Science,* August 24, 1934.

advantage one should go by way of Barstow and Silver Lake and return through Darwin and Lone Pine. If one desires a dash of human interest, he can visit some of the old mining-camps, settle down for a few days at a place such as Ballarat or Darwin, and get acquainted with some of the good-natured inhabitants of those out-of-the-way corners of the desert domain.

From Palm Springs or Indio the vacationist can reach the Salton Sea, the mud-volcanoes, the beautiful sandstone and clay hills to the east of Mecca, the rolling dunes near Yuma; and, nearer at hand, the scenic, palm-inhabited canyons of Mount San Jacinto.

On the Los Angeles–Lone Pine tour one sees to advantage large joshua - tree forests, the magnificent erosional forms of Red Rock Canyon, spacious dry lakes, tinted volcanic craters and black lava flows, and, at last, Owens Lake, the escarpment of the Inyo Range, and the steep granite wall of the majestic Sierra Nevada.

The journey to Needles acquaints one with the broad depressions of the mid-Mohave region, its strange, picturesque, fan-encircled mountain forms, black cinder cones, and recent lava flows, and the broad flood plains of the Colorado River.

The principal points of interest on the Las Vegas road are the vari-tinted Calico Mountains; the Lake Manix clay beds; the magnificent Cima Dome; Soda Lake; and, as the California border is reached, the strange mountains of banded limestones.

A large area of about one million acres, for the most part in Riverside County, was early in 1937 set aside as the Joshua Tree National Monument. It embraces a wide variety of biological environments ranging from near sea level to 5,000-

feet altitude. Its plants and animals are of both Great Basin
and Sonoran affinities and represent many species not found
in the more northern Death Valley Monument. The area is
one of splendid scenic beauty with remarkable rock formations, deep canyons, and broad desert basins. From Inspira-
tion Point one gains a comprehensive view of the marvelous
Salton Basin such as can be gained from few other eminences.
A week or an entire month spent here in spring or autumn
will yield rich rewards to the intelligent traveler.

Since one knows intimately only the country he has
walked over, take my hint: abandon the motor car as soon as
possible and travel on foot. Then you will move in a leisurely
manner, confine your wanderings to a small area, and enter
into profitable intimacy with nature. Go alone on your walks
if you can, but if you must take a companion, choose one
who will appreciate with you the desert's great silence.

Early in the day when the senses are keen and fresh, take
to climbing the mountains. The higher you climb, the more
marvelous is the prospect. The country now acquires new
importance, and every mountain range seen in the distance
invites exploration.

SELECTED REFERENCES

AUSTIN, MARY. *Land of Little Rain*, Houghton Mifflin, 1903.

BAILEY, VERNON. "Harmful and Beneficial Mammals of the Arid Interior," *United States Department of Agriculture Farmers Bulletin No. 335*, 1908.

———. "Sources of Water Supply for Desert Animals," *Scientific Monthly*, XVII (1923), 66–86.

BROWN, J. S. "Routes to Desert Watering Places in the Salton Sea Region, California," *United States Geological Survey Water-Supply Paper 490-A*, 1920.

BUXTON, P. A. *Animal Life in Deserts*, E. Arnold & Co., London, 1923.

CAMP, C. L. "Notes on the Local Distribution and Habits of the Amphibians and Reptiles of Southeastern California in the Vicinity of the Turtle Mountains," *University of California Publications in Zoölogy*, XII (1916), 503–43.

CAMPBELL, ELIZABETH W. CROZER. "An Archeological Survey of the Twenty-nine Palms Region," *Southwest Museum Papers, No. 7*, 1931.

———. "Pinto Basin Site, An Ancient Aboriginal Camping Ground in the California Desert," *Southwest Museum Papers, No. 9*, 1935.

CANNON, W. A. *Root Habits of Desert Plants*, Carnegie Institution of Washington, Washington, D.C., 1911.

CARTER, FRANCIS. "Bird Life at Twenty-nine Palms," *The Condor*, Vol. XXXIX (1937), No. 5.

CHASE, J. S. *California Desert Trails*, Houghton Mifflin, 1919.

COUES, ELLIOT. *Birds of the Colorado Valley*, Government Printing Office, Washington, D.C., 1878.

COVILLE, F. V. "Botany of the Death Valley Expedition," *Contributions from the United States National Herbarium, No. 4*, 1893.

COWLES, RAYMOND B. "Notes on the Ecology and Breeding Habits of the Desert Minnow, *Cyprinodon macularius*," *Copeia, No. 1*, 1934.

DARTON, N. H., AND OTHERS. "Guidebook of the Western United States, Part C, Santa Fe Route," *United States Geological Survey Bulletin 613*, 1916.

DAVIS, WM. MORRIS. "Basin Range Types," *Science,* LXXVI (1932), 241–45.

——. "Granitic Domes of the Mohave Desert, California," *Transactions of the San Diego Society of Natural History,* Vol. VII (1933), No. 20, pp. 211–58.

GALE, H. S. "Salines in the Owens, Searles, and Panamint Basins, Southeastern California," *United States Geological Survey Bulletin 580,* 1915, pp. 251–323.

GRINNELL, JOSEPH. "An Account of the Mammals and Birds of the Lower Colorado Valley," *University of California Publications in Zoölogy,* Vol. XV (1915).

——. "Further Observations upon the Bird Life of Death Valley," *The Condor,* Vol. XXXVI, March 1934.

HARDER, E. C. "Iron-Ore Deposits of the Eagle Mountains, California," *United States Geological Survey Bulletin 503,* 1912.

HERRE, A. W. C. T. "Lichens, Impossible Plants," *Scientific Monthly,* Vol. XVI (1923), No. 2, pp. 130–40.

HOFFMAN, RALPH. *Birds of the Pacific States,* Houghton Mifflin, 1927.

HORNADAY, W. T. *Campfires on Desert and Lava,* Scribner's, 1908.

HUNTINGTON, ELLSWORTH. *Civilization and Climate,* Yale University Press, 1924.

KLAUBER, L. M. "A Key to the Rattlesnakes with Summary of Characteristics," *Transactions of the San Diego Society of Natural History,* Vol. VIII (1936), No. 20.

LAWSON, A. C. "The Epigene Profiles of the Desert," *University of California Department of Geology Bulletin,* IX (1915), 37–38.

LONGWELL, CHESTER, KNOPF, ADOLPH, AND FLINT, RICHARD. *A Textbook of Geology,* John Wiley & Sons, 1932.

LOUDERBACK, GEO. D. "Basin Range Structure in the Great Basin," *University of California Publications in Geology,* Vol. XIV (1923), No. 10.

LOUDERMILK, J. D. "On the Origin of Desert Varnish," *American Journal of Science,* XXI (1931), 51–65.

MACDOUGAL, D. T., *Botanical Features of North American Deserts,* Carnegie Institution of Washington, Washington, D.C., 1908.

MALLERY, T. D. "Rainfall Records for the Sonoran Desert," *Ecology,* Nos. 1 and 2, 1936.

McKELVEY, SUSAN DELANO. "Notes on Yucca," *Journal of the Arnold Arboretum,* Vol. XVI, 1935.

MANLY, W. L. *Death Valley in '49,* Pacific Tree and Vine Company, San Jose, 1894.

MEINZER, O. E. "Map of the Pleistocene Lakes of the Basin and Range Province and Its Significance," *Bulletin of the Geological Society of America,* XXXIII (1922), 541–52.

MENDENHALL, W. C. "Groundwaters of the Indio Region, California, with a Sketch of the Colorado Desert," *United States Geological Survey Water-Supply Paper 225,* 1909.

———. "Some Desert Watering Places in Southeastern California and Southwestern Nevada," *United States Geological Survey Water-Supply Paper 224,* 1909.

MERRIAM, J. C. "Extinct Faunas of the Mohave Desert," *Popular Science,* LXXXVI (1915), 245–64.

MILLER, LOYE. "Notes on the Desert Tortoise," *Transactions of the San Diego Society of Natural History,* Vol. VII (1932), No. 18.

MOSAUER, WALTER. "The Reptiles of a Sand Dune Area and Its Surroundings in the Colorado Desert," *Ecology,* Vol. XVI (1935), No. 1.

NOBLE, L. F. "Note on a Colemanite Deposit near Shoshone, California, with a Sketch of a Part of Amargosa Valley," *United States Geological Survey Bulletin 785,* 1926.

PARISH, S. B. "Vegetation of the Mohave and Colorado Deserts of Southern California," *Ecology,* Vol. XI (1930), No. 3.

ROGERS, MALCOLM J. "Report of an Archaeological Reconnaissance in the Mohave Sink Region," *Archeology,* Vol. I (1929), No. 1.

———. "Yuman Pottery Making," *San Diego Museum Papers, No. 2,* 1936.

SAUNDERS, CHARLES F. *The Southern Sierras of California,* Houghton Mifflin, 1923.

SHREVE, FOREST. "The Plant Life of the Sonoran Desert," *The Scientific Monthly,* March 1936.

———. "The Problems of the Desert," *The Scientific Monthly,* March 1934.

SHREVE, FOREST, AND MALLERY, T. D. "The Relation of Caliche to Desert Plants," *Soil Science,* Vol. XXXV (1933), No. 2.

SPAULDING, V. M. *Distribution and Movements of Desert Plants,* Carnegie Institution of Washington, Washington, D.C., 1909.

SPURR, J. E. "Descriptive Geology of Nevada South of the Fortieth Parallel and Adjacent Portions of California," *United States Geological Survey Bulletin 208,* 1903.

SUMNER, F. B. "Some Biological Problems of Our Southwestern Deserts," *Ecology,* VI (1925), 352–71.

THORPE, W. H. "Miscellaneous Records of Insects Inhabiting the Saline Waters of the California Desert Regions," *Pan-Pacific Entomologist,* Vol. VII (1931), No. 4.

TIDESTROM, I. "Flora of Utah and Nevada," *Contributions from the United States National Herbarium, No. 25,* 1925.

THOMPSON, DAVID G. "The Mohave Desert Region, California," *United States Geological Survey Water-Supply Paper 578,* 1929.

VORHIES, C. T. "Poisonous Animals of the Desert," *Arizona University Agricultural Experiment Station Bulletin, No. 83,* 1917.

VAN DYKE, J. C. *Desert: Further Studies in Natural Appearances,* Scribner's, 1901.

WARING, G. A. "Ground-Water in Pahrump and Ivanpah Valleys, Nevada and California," *United States Geological Survey Water-Supply Paper 450,* 1920.

WALTHER, J. *Das Gesetz der Wüstenbildung* (4th edition), Leipzig, 1924.

INDEX

203

Jaeger, Edmund Carroll, 1887–

The California deserts; a visitor's handbook, by Edmund
C. Jaeger; with chapters by S. Stillman Berry and Malcolm
J. Rogers. Rev. ed. ... Stanford University, Calif., Stanford university press; London, H. Milford, Oxford university press [1948, c1938]

x, 209 p. illus. 20 cm.

Maps on lining-papers.
"The area here treated embraces both the Mohave ... and the Colorado desert of southeastern California and also certain contiguous portions of southern Nevada and western Arizona."—Introd.
"Selected references": p. 199–202.

1. California, Southern—Descr. & trav. 2. Deserts. 3. Mohave
desert, Calif. 4. Colorado   desert, Calif. 5. Natural history—
California, Southern.   I. Berry, Samuel Stillman, 1887–
II. Rogers, Malcolm   Jennings, 1890–   III. Title.
Library of Congress   F867.J232   38—3543

                                  [50k1]   [551.58]   917.949